Darden Business Publishing Presents

THE
STRATEGIST'S
TOOLKIT

By Jared D. Harris and Michael J. Lenox

DARDEN
BUSINESS PUBLISHING
UNIVERSITY *of* VIRGINIA

Darden Business Publishing
Darden School of Business
University of Virginia

Harris, Jared D. and Michael J. Lenox, authors.
The Strategist's Toolkit / Jared D. Harris and Michael J. Lenox.
Includes bibliographical references.
ISBN 978-1-61598-197-7

*To our students, who have inspired us
and taught us over the years.*

*To our colleagues, who have helped us better
articulate many of these ideas.*

*And to our families, who have tirelessly
supported and sustained us.*

Contents

PART 4. PUTTING IT ALL TOGETHER

Preface

The *Strategist's Toolkit* is a unique resource for helping students, managers, and executives in strategic analysis and decision making. The toolkit lays out a collection of tools and frameworks to help you perform a strategic analysis of a business enterprise, and decide upon and justify a proper course of action.

The toolkit is not a substitute for a textbook or case collection, although it could be usefully employed in concert with a textbook or series of cases. Whereas a textbook might contain detailed theoretical treatments of important concepts, the *Strategist's Toolkit* instead strives to lay out brief, useful explanations of analytical tools that can be readily integrated and employed to evaluate a competitive situation. The toolkit is action-oriented and is designed to make the underlying strategic frameworks accessible and easy to use. While an extended treatment of strategy's intellectual underpinnings has been left to the existing extensive collection of texts and articles, we have attempted to build on those fundamental ideas in summarizing and presenting these frameworks. In that sense, the *Strategist's Toolkit* constitutes an easy-to-digest primer on the fundamental building blocks of strategic analysis.

This allows the toolkit to be useful in a variety of situations, either alone or in combination with other resources. This allows you—the student, manager, or executive—to use the toolkit in a way that is most meaningful and useful to you: to help you analyze a competitive situation your own firm faces; to supplement a text or other source of theoretical content; as frameworks to employ in analyzing a case or series of cases; in a course on strategic management or strategic thinking; or as a supplemental reference work in either your professional or academic endeavors.

The organization of the *Strategist's Toolkit* is straightforward. The first chapter provides an overview of conducting an integrative strategic analysis. The remaining chapters focus on specific tools that are useful as building blocks in conducting a strategic analysis. A glossary of terms frequently encountered in strategy discussions and a table of common strategy analytics are included at the end of the book.

We would like to acknowledge the contributions of many of our colleagues, to whom we are indebted for their help in the development of the toolkit. Indeed, the initial efforts to develop some of the material were not originally conceived as components of an integrated reference guide but rather as standalone, brief technical notes. Only over time did it become apparent how an integrated collection of these frameworks would prove useful to instructors and students alike. Many conversations that (in retrospect) served as important origins for chapters in the toolkit occurred during teaching meetings of faculty teaching the required strategy course in the first-year curriculum of the University of Virginia's Darden School of Business, our home institution, over the course of the past six years. Therefore, we are especially indebted to the Darden School faculty constituting those teaching teams over the years: Jay Bourgeois, Ming-Jer Chen, Greg Fairchild, Ed Freeman, Jeanne Liedtka, Scott Snell, and San-karan Venkataraman.

In addition, there are many colleagues who have made particularly substantive contributions. Chapter 5 draws directly from the work of Ed Hess. Chapter 6 summarizes the work of Ed Freeman and Andy Wicks on stakeholder theory, a set of ideas that comes with breathing the air at the Darden School. The ideas in Chapter 7 were largely developed and championed by Scott Snell, who helped us understand firm capabilities in a new way. Chapter 10 draws heavily from the work of Jeanne Liedtka, who was invaluable in articulating the concepts of hypothesis testing. The Darden School's reference librarian, Susan Norrisey, helped write the appendix "Gathering Strategic Intelligence," and Scott Rockart of University of North Carolina's Kenan-Flagler Business School contributed to the appendix "Strategy Analytics."

We are also, in a general sense, deeply indebted to the Darden School as an institution, which provides an invigorating intellectual environment in which to work every day. We cannot imagine a better place to explore the idea of integrative analytical frameworks than the Darden School, which exists to "improve the world" by "advancing knowledge" and "developing and inspiring responsible leaders." In our teaching, we strive to help our students embrace an enterprise perspective; in our research, we seek to develop ideas that make a difference in the world. The development of this book is entirely consistent with these institutional objectives. In some small way, we hope to have conveyed the integrative spirit of the Darden School in the *Strategist's Toolkit*.

Our hope is that the *Strategist's Toolkit* will provide you with an organized, succinct guide for conducting a strategic analysis.

1. Introduction to Strategic Analysis[i]

Every organization needs a strategy. Be it an established business, an emerging entrepreneurial venture, or a nonprofit organization, a strategy sets the direction of the enterprise, informs priorities and the allocation of scarce resources, and helps guide the myriad decisions that an organization makes every day.

But what exactly is *strategy?* Kenneth Andrews provides the following definition:

> [S]trategy is the pattern of decisions in a company that determines and reveals its objectives, purposes, or goals, produces the principal policies and plans for achieving those goals, and defines the range of business the company is to pursue, the kind of economic and human organization it is or intends to be, and the nature of the economic and noneconomic contribution it intends to make to its shareholders, employees, customers, and communities.[ii]

Such a definition of strategy highlights its complex nature. Strategy encompasses several different sets of considerations. An organization's strategic goals or objectives refer to the organization's *mission,* its unique purpose and scope. The strategic plan, sometimes called strategic *intent,* is how the organization tailors its offerings and develops and leverages internal resources and capabilities to accomplish strategic goals. Strategic *actions* are those tangible actions taken to operationalize the strategic plan in pursuit of the strategic goals of the business.

Together, this triad of mission, intent, and actions defines an organization's strategy. They reveal how an organization creates unique value for its customers and other stakeholders, and how it distinctively positions itself relative to other organizations in its field.

Understanding and assessing an organization's strategy is critically important to many organizational constituents. One need not be the CEO, president, or a member of the top management team to engage in such analysis. Consultants, investment bankers, entrepreneurs, and others frequently must assess the strategy of firms, whether they are their own businesses, clients', or competitors'. Managers, consultants, and analysts are frequently asked to identify and assess the strategy of a business or an organization. Whether it is to properly value a business or acquisition target, undertake a new corporate initiative, or enter a new market, one needs an understanding of an organization's strategy to formulate an informed and robust recommendation.

The purpose of this book is to provide an organized framework and a set of tools to aid those who wish to analyze the strategy of an organization, whether it's their own or another organization they are interested in. This book explains a number of the basic tools necessary to be an effective strategic analyst or strategist, an individual skilled in the art of assessing an organization's strategy. Strategic analysis is a powerful tool for analyzing the competitive context in which an organization operates. An effective strategist makes reasoned and reasonable recommendations for how an organization should position itself relative to its peers and for assessing what actions the organization should take to maximize value creation for its various stakeholders. While our bias is toward analysis of business organizations operating in market environments (e.g., corporations, small- and medium-size businesses, entrepreneurial ventures), the tools presented here could be applied to organizations in the nonprofit and governmental spheres (e.g., schools, advocacy groups, community organizations, municipal governments).

The Strategist's Challenge

The strategist's challenge is to balance the intersection between three critical factors: values, opportunities, and capabilities (**Figure 1-1**).

Figure 1-1. The strategist's challenge.

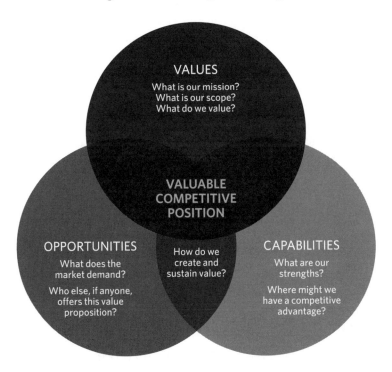

Values refer to the mission of the organization. What is the organization's purpose, its reason for existing? What is the organization's scope; in what markets or arenas does the organization operate? What do the organization's various stakeholders expect of the organization? What do the organization's leaders expect of the enterprise? What values and beliefs does the organization hold? The answers to these questions are critical for understanding the strategy of an organization and provide the baseline for any strategic analysis. Indeed, the most fundamental question a strategist must initially ask and understand is: what are the organization's values? An understanding of firm values is the foundation that can give meaning and provide context to the strategic decisions an organization makes.

Opportunities refer to the potential to create value for stakeholders. What does the market demand? What needs may be identified? Who else in the market is satisfying these needs? There are a variety of external forces—competitive, economic, and technological—that influence an organization's opportunity set. Factors such as the rapid development of information and communication technologies, the increased global reach of businesses, the multinational distribution of labor pools and supply chains, and the worldwide interest and influence of stakeholders of all types have all had a profound impact on the opportunities facing organizations. The strategist requires clear thinking about the economic, technological, and societal environment in which the organization operates as well as an acute consideration of the activities and capabilities of one's competitors.

Capabilities refer to the organization's existing and potential strengths. To evaluate an organization's strategy, one must have both a clear picture of what makes the organization distinctive and a sense of the organization's ability to marshal resources and leverage capabilities toward desired organizational objectives. This requires, of course, clarity about organizational capabilities: What capabilities do we currently possess? Are these capabilities unique and do they provide the basis for a competitive advantage? What capabilities do we need to possess in the future? How will we develop them?

The challenge for the strategist is to balance these three factors and identify the space where they converge. It is at the intersection of values, opportunities, and capabilities that valuable competitive positions that create and sustain value for stakeholders emerge.

Ultimately, strategic analysis is an *integrative* exercise. Whereas the functional areas of an organization—finance, marketing, accounting, operations, human resources—often bring specific paradigmatic views to bear on organizational problems and considerations, strategy is about how all the underlying insights of these disciplines are brought back together. Managers do not typically encounter challenges as isolated, atomistic problems with narrow disciplinary implications; rather, they must navigate issues encompassing a whole range of complex, cross-disciplinary considerations.

Strategy is also integrative in the sense that its success involves value creation for its investors, employees, customers, suppliers, and communities. Commonly invoked business axioms such as "maximize shareholder returns" can be useful to the extent that such shorthand phrases imply value creation for investors *by way of* creating value for key stakeholders—creating goods customers want, work environments that energize employee contributions, and so forth. But shareholder profit maximization as an organization's formal objective provides little strategic direction if it implies adherence to the naïve notion that shareholder value is somehow exogenous to creating value for customers or employees or communities. Strategy involves putting these considerations together in an attempt to align stakeholder interests and create value in an integrative and sustainable way.

At the same time, tradeoffs must sometimes be made, and a strategist often faces difficult choices. Tradeoffs between costs and quality and between various customer segments are frequently confronted when considering strategy. The most difficult strategic tradeoffs are often temporal, as between strategic long-term investments and short-term performance. An integrative, enterprise perspective is necessary to think clearly and to exercise sound judgment about how to best create long-lasting value. Individual analytical frameworks and tools, grounded in both theory and practice, can help, although any device used to help analyze strategic problems will prove insightful in some ways but blunt in others. The key to strategic analysis is to integrate these frameworks and tools to form a comprehensive understanding of the competitive context in which the organization operates.

The Art of Strategic Analysis

Strategic analysis can be a powerful tool when executed well. Effective analyses explore the competitive situation, define key issues, recognize critical assumptions and tradeoffs, and propose strategically sensible recommendations. In any analysis, it is important to be prepared to articulate your major conclusions and provide evidence and analysis in support of them. You should be prepared to not only present your own analysis and conclusions but also to respectively challenge and extend the viewpoints of others. There is rarely one wrong or right answer to a strategic analysis, and yet, some answers are assuredly better than others. Thus, strategic analysis requires the honing of your skill in logic and argumentation, so that you can advance your hypothesis or viewpoint and logically provide support through both qualitative and quantitative analysis.

Even in the most ambiguous scenarios, it is important to examine whatever data is available as well as your key reasoning and assumptions that make some recommendations better than others (see sidebar, Gathering Strategic Intelligence). Once research is undertaken, one of the challenges of strategic analysis is to pull from the diverse and often incomplete data available to support your arguments and conclusions. Strategic analyses are far more focused, productive, and persuasive when informed and supported by specific data and quantitative analysis. Similarly, quantitative analysis, no matter how elegant, is far more reliable and robust when critiqued within a broader strategic context that involves a range of relevant considerations that are more difficult to quantify.

Data and quantitative analyses may be used to focus discussion by identifying key issues and to back up arguments. Calculations should be conducted, therefore, in the context of specific questions or beliefs. For example, deciding whether or not to make a particular acquisition should be guided by such fundamental questions as, "How will the combined enterprise be better positioned to create value?" and, "How will we create that value?" In turn, believing that an acquisition is very important leads us to ask, "How much of an effect would the acquisition have on the market value of the firm?" and perhaps, "How much will market prices fall if competitors made the acquisition instead?" If the focus of an analysis revolves around a risky investment, you may want to quickly calculate the net present value of the investment and do a sensitivity analysis to identify a few key uncertainties for discussion. This might entail predicting the future discounted cash flows that will result from a given strategic action. Alternatively, you might calculate the break-even for the investment or, recognizing that the risky investment can be made in stages, put together a decision tree that shows the possible outcomes and values at each stage.

Of course, any calculation is simply a reorganization of available information; as such, calculations are not insightful on their own. But quantitative analyses can *support* a larger strategic analysis that *does* shed light on key issues in a particular situation. For instance, a simple ratio (e.g., return on assets) may transform some raw numbers about competitors into a clear picture of which firms are outperforming their rivals and why those firms are doing better. Alternatively, a few calculations may transform ratios and raw numbers (e.g., spending per person and number of consumers in the segment) back into data that may be more relevant to certain key decisions (e.g., total market size). Because such calculations are often necessary but not sufficient for good strategic analysis, you should be prepared to discuss any relevant financial data, but also be ready to discuss the relevance of that data to the key strategic issues under consideration.

At the end of this toolkit, we provide a list of common financial measures and mathematical tools that may be useful when analyzing a firm's strategy. The list is not intended to be a comprehensive treatment of these tools; rather, it is intended to summarize, remind, and encourage you to apply your existing knowledge when conducting strategy research.

A Framework for Strategic Analysis

At the very least, a full-blown strategic analysis includes (1) an identification of the organization's current competitive positioning and an assessment of the strengths and weaknesses of that position, (2) a consideration of the pros and cons of a relatively small set of strategic actions to help improve that position, and (3) the advancement of a set of recommendations based on this analysis. Collected in this toolkit are a number of common frameworks and tools that are useful when conducting such a three-part analysis. Note that none of the tools presented is sufficient, in and of itself, for conducting a strategic analysis. The tools *work together* to paint a complete picture of the competitive context of an organization. The key to an effective strategic analysis is the *integration* of these tools into a compelling argument for action moving forward. Many of the tools included here are most useful as "back office" support to your analysis rather than as an end product. In other words, a client or boss for whom you are preparing a strategic analysis is less concerned about seeing that you conducted a five forces analysis or stakeholder analysis than the actual insights you gain from completing these analyses and how those insights influence your recommendations. As such, you may only perform them in the back office to advance your own thinking and analysis.

As a way to organize these tools, it may be useful to think of a classic strategic analysis framework, the SWOT analysis. SWOT stands for strengths, weaknesses, opportunities, and threats. Although perhaps the most basic of all strategic frameworks, SWOT emphasizes two main components of any strategic analysis: consideration of the external competitive environment (opportunities and threats) and the internal strengths and weaknesses of the focal organization under scrutiny. This interplay between external and internal is at the heart of any good strategic analysis. Some tools, such as competitor analysis, environmental analysis, and five forces analysis, are useful for understanding the external competitive environment. Others, such as capabilities analysis and diversification matrices, are useful for understanding the internal strengths and weaknesses of the firm. Still others, such as strategic maps and stakeholder analysis, are useful in combining external and internal assessments and understanding the positioning of an organization among its peers and competitors. Finally others, such as scenario analysis and payoff matrices, are useful to consider how the dynamics of competition effect strategic positioning.

The remainder of the toolkit is organized into three parts. Part 1 presents a collection of tools that help with the analysis of the external competitive environment, the opportunities portion of the strategist's challenge. These tools will help you answer questions such as: What industry is the organization in and who are the players in this industry? Is this an attractive industry? Are there barriers to competition? What are the major trends impacting this industry? How is the competitive structure of the industry likely to evolve? What is the underlying competitive game being played?

Part 2 presents a collection of tools that help with the analysis of competitive position highlighting both the capabilities portion of the strategist's challenge and the integration across values, opportunities, and capabilities. These tools will help you answer questions such as: Who are the organization's relevant stakeholders and what do they expect of the organization? How does the organization create value for its stakeholders? What are the organization's unique resources and capabilities? How sustainable is any advantage the organization may have from these assets? Can the organization leverage these assets across markets in order to improve its position in a market? Given all this, how should the organization position itself in the market relative to its rivals? How can the organization secure and sustain favorable positions over time?

Part 3 presents a collection of tools that aid in the analysis of specific strategic decisions and provide guidance on how to assess whether a potential action will improve an organization's creation of value. These tools will help you answer questions such as: How can we best improve the position of the organization in its competitive environment? How will competitors react to specific strategic actions? What is the value in investing in various opportunities and building certain capabilities? What potential futures may the organization face and what is the value of specific actions in each of those futures? Ultimately, these tools provide guidance for recommending specific strategic actions.

We conclude with Chapter 15, "Strategic Analysis in Practice," where we return to our discussion about integration and discuss a step-by-step process to conduct a strategic analysis utilizing the various tools in the toolkit.

Ultimately, executing a well-done strategic analysis is a skill that requires application and will develop over time through repetition. An expert strategist can conduct a compelling analysis in a number of situations: the multiweek project, the rapid follow-up to an urgent late-night call from the client looking for quick suggestions, or even the elevator ride with the boss who asks for thoughts on some pressing strategic issue facing the organization. The tools in this toolkit provide the foundation on which to conduct a strategic analysis in all its forms. The key is to integrate these frameworks and tools into a compelling argument and analysis.

One of the biggest challenges of any strategic analysis involve (1) gathering information, (2) determining which pieces of that information/data are useful and relevant, and (3) employing gathered information as part of a fruitful strategic analysis. You are often challenged with either too much or not enough information. The big question is often how to find and utilize the right data. Fortunately, there are many resources at your disposal to help gather data on particular organizations and industries.

There are a number of places you might look for information relevant to your analysis that are available to anyone on the Internet. For example, an obvious place to start is an organization's own website and its most recent annual report. You might pay attention to recent media coverage of a certain organization or industry as you regularly read business papers, publications, and blogs, especially pertaining to the organization's strategy and competitive position. Certain hard-copy publications, such as the industry surveys of Standard & Poor's, can be found in research libraries. Industry surveys provide useful information on market share and sector-specific issues and are updated up to several times a year. Value Line's loose-leaf print publications also provide detailed information on 1,500 stocks in roughly 100 industry groups, updated quarterly. Value Line updates industry sector reports weekly and can be found in research libraries or larger public libraries. In addition to such print resources, there are a number of online research databases and resources available through university subscription that you might also find helpful as you gather relevant information.

You should search in various publications for articles and news items that touch directly or indirectly on the industry and company you have selected. A good place to start is by searching through the library indexes and databases for your industry and company. You should attempt to locate articles that go back several years, rather than focus exclusively upon the most recent ones. Try to begin with magazine articles that may provide more general background information before you consult newspapers that deal with specific recent developments. Business or trade publications and company documents filed with the SEC will provide you with even more useful information. The Internet is a valuable resource for collecting information but please proceed wisely. The information that is posted on the Internet varies widely in terms of its validity and quality; pay the most attention to information posted by the firms themselves, established news or media firms, and universities. You should be able to find a wealth of information even if you limit yourself to these sources. We summarize a number of specific research databases that may be useful for conducting research in support of analyzing a firm's strategy at the end of this book.

PART 1.

Tools for Analyzing the Competitive Environment

2. Competitor Analysis

What is it?

Competitor analysis is a framework for understanding and evaluating current or potential competitors of a firm. While deceptively simple—and typically only an initial step in a robust strategic analysis—a competitor analysis is an indispensable tool in any strategist's toolkit.

When do we use it?

While competitor analysis is by nature only one component of a more robust strategic analysis that employs multiple frameworks and tools, it can be a useful starting point for thinking about competitive dynamics and analyzing the industry in greater detail. It helps identify the most relevant competitors and gives a baseline understanding of how those firms compete.

Why do we use it?

A good strategic analysis requires a careful analysis of the firm's competition in order to assess and predict the durability of any competitive advantage, including the potential response of rivals to various strategic actions the firm may be considering. Competitor analysis can help firms make better-informed strategic decisions and gather competitive intelligence on the industry. A thorough competitor analysis can even help firms recognize opportunities to influence their rivals' behavior to their own advantage.

When assessing a firm's strategy and its capacity to create value for important stakeholders, keep in mind the fundamental principle of competition: If everyone can do it, it is difficult to create value from it. Strategy plays out in a competitive arena. How will competitors react to the strategic actions of a business? Will competitors be able to easily imitate those moves? How will other stakeholders—say, customers or the community—respond? Strategy must be formulated and implemented "with an appreciation of these second-order effects."[iii]

As a simple illustration of this fundamental principle of competition, consider a vendor, Kate, selling T-shirts outside the University of Virginia's basketball arena. Suppose this vendor does quite well for herself selling a quality T-shirt at a reasonable markup over costs; her enterprise provides a good return for the vendor and a product that customers find desirable. But how do others respond? Absent any barriers to entry and attracted by the opportunity, other T-shirt vendors may also soon appear outside the arena. Absent any barriers to imitation, they may, in fact, sell exact replicas of the T-shirts Kate is currently selling. As the supply of T-shirts increases, the competition for customers also increases, and vendors may start lowering their prices to attract customers. Soon enough, prices may fall to the point that the next potential entrepreneur, Jack, elects not to enter the parking lot T-shirt market because the opportunity cost is too high and his next best option for a business venture is more attractive than becoming a T-shirt vendor. The remaining vendors may be currently profiting from their ventures, but such profits may not exceed their opportunity cost. This is what economists refer to as *economic profit* or *economic rents*. It differs from accounting profit in that it refers to profits in excess of the opportunity cost of capital. In practical terms, the question for entrepreneurs is whether they can create more value entering a different market instead.

The fundamental principle of competition suggests that a successful strategy requires some barrier to competition that prevents others from entering a firm's market and imitating its strategy. In the case of Kate the T-shirt vendor, restrictions that require permission to sell outside the arena, in the form of a license or permit, could serve as a barrier to entry. Copyright and trademarks could serve as barriers to imitation of Kate's T-shirt designs. Together, barriers to entry and barriers to imitation can reduce competitive pressures and allow our T-shirt vendor to thrive. Only in the presence of such barriers to competition can a firm be expected to earn a stream of economic profits in the future. A thorough strategic analysis—one that identifies and analyzes the firm's direct competitors—can therefore help one forecast future cash flows for a firm and thus calculate an expected market value for the firm.

How do we use it?

Step 1. Identify competitors.

While seemingly straightforward, competitor identification is a critical and often challenging first step in a competitor analysis. Two companies in the same industry may vary significantly in the degree to which they compete. They may compete in different geographic markets or target radically different customer segments. For example, is an analysis of Kia, a builder of low-cost sedans, useful to Porsche, a luxury sports car manufacturer? In some cases, even identifying a company's industry can be difficult.

There are two common ways to identify competition. The first is to look at the industry from a customer's viewpoint and group all firms providing a similar product or service. Marketers have developed various techniques such as perception mapping and brand-switching analyses to aid in identifying the most relevant competitors. Point-of-sales and scanner data provide rich sources to help with these analyses. The gold standard is to identify the cross-price elasticity between pairs of products (i.e., the percentage increase in demand for one product given a percentage decrease in price for another product). The larger the increase in demand, the more two products are substitutes, and their makers are rivals. In practice, however, cross-price elasticity can be difficult to calculate.

The second approach is to carry out a detailed analysis of industry players and group firms with similar strategies as competitors. For example, if analyzing the U.S. steel industry, it may be useful to classify companies into three strategic groups: large integrated steel mills, minimills (which use a different technology), and foreign importers. It may also be worthwhile to collect data on those who provide related products; for example, aluminum and plastic manufacturers as alternative competitors in the case of the steel industry. By clustering competitors into strategic groups, you can prioritize your intelligence gathering, focusing first and foremost on those rivals most closely related to the focal firm while also being cognizant of more distant competitors. Strategic group identification can be a quick and easy approach in many situations.

Step 2. Gather intelligence.

Once the competition has been identified, data can be gathered to provide insight on the competitor(s). These include historical data such as shareholder reports or SEC filings as well as press releases, media coverage, interviews with analysts and managers, and public relations events. Recent performance, existing strategies, and organizational capabilities can also be studied by examining the firm's hiring activity and patterns, research and development activity, capital investments, and strategic partnerships.

Competitor information can be pulled together in a simple spreadsheet (**Figure 2-1**):

Figure 2-1. Competitor information spreadsheet.

	REVENUES	MARKET SHARE	ROA	R&D INVESTMENT	STRATEGIC PARTNERSHIPS
Focal Firm					
Strategic Group 1					
Competitor 1					
Competitor 2					
Competitor 3					
Competitor 4					
Strategic Group 2					
Competitor 1					
Competitor 2					
Competitor 3					
Competitor 4					
Strategic Group 3					
Competitor 1					
Competitor 2					
Competitor 3					
Competitor 4					

Step 3. Analyze rivals.

The final step is analyzing the competitive positions of rivals and comparing their relative strengths and weaknesses. The simple diagram in **Figure 2-2** is a useful guidepost for thinking about competitive responses. First, what drives a given competitor? What are its objectives and its operating assumptions?

Second, what is the competitor capable of doing? How do its strategy, resources, and capabilities allow it to compete now and in the future?

While this last part of a competitor analysis is the most subjective, it can provide useful insights into the sustainability of a focal firm's competitive advantage and how competitors may respond to specific strategic actions by the focal firm.

Figure 2-2. Competitor positions.

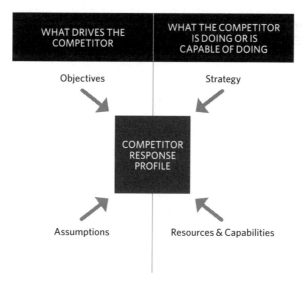

Adapted from Michael E. Porter, *Competitive Strategy.*

||||||||||||||||||||||||||||||||||||||||||||||||||||||||||||||||||||||||||

FOUNDATIONAL READINGS

Caves, R. E., and M.E. Porter. "From Entry Barriers to Mobility Barriers: Conjectural Decisions and Contrived Deterrence to New Competition." *Quarterly Journal of Economics* 91 (1977): 241–61.

Chen, Ming-Jer. "Competitor Analysis and Interfirm Rivalry: Toward a Theoretical Integration." *Academy of Management Review* 21 (1996): 100–34.

Fiegenbaum, A., and H. Thomas. "Strategic Groups as Reference Groups: Theory, Modeling and Empirical Examination of Industry and Competitive Strategy." *Strategic Management Journal* (1995): 16.

Ghemawat, P. "Sustainable Advantage." *Harvard Business Review* 86 (1986): 53–58.

Grant, R. *Contemporary Strategic Analysis.* Oxford: Blackwell Publishers, 2008.

Lippman, S., and R. P. Rumelt. "Uncertain Imitability: An Analysis of Interfirm Differences in Efficiency under Competition." *Bell Journal of Economics* 13 (1982): 418–38.

Peteraf, M., and M. Bergen. "Scanning Dynamic Competitive Landscapes: A Market-Based and Resource-Based Framework." *Strategic Management Journal* 24 (2003): 1027–041.

Porter, M. *Competitive Strategy: Techniques for Analyzing Industries and Competitors.* New York: Free Press, 1980.

Williamson, 0. E. *The Economic Institutions of Capitalism.* New York: Free Press, 1985.

Zajac, E. J., and M. H. Bazerman. "Blind Spots in Industry and Competitor Analysis: Implications of Interfirm (Mis)Perceptions for Strategic Decisions." *Academy of Management Review* 16 (1991): 37–56.

3. Environmental Analysis

What is it?

Environmental analysis (sometimes referred to as "environmental scanning") is the analysis of factors in the larger competitive context that are currently affecting or may in the future influence the nature of competition within an industry.

When do we use it?

Environmental analysis identifies trends that influence things such as demand, growth, entry and exit of firms, innovation, and regulation. Environmental analysis can lead to better planning and decision making for a firm but should be used in combination with other analytical tools.

Why do we use it?

While constituting a simple framework for organizing data and observations about the larger societal context, environmental analysis can nevertheless be a useful starting point for thinking about institutional and environmental factors that impact the firm's strategic actions.

Although the competitive prospects for a firm are directly influenced by the competitive actions and strategic options of its competitors (as addressed in a competitor analysis), a number of broader societal forces can also impact the opportunities a firm has for creating value for its stakeholders. For instance, a typewriter manufacturing firm in the late 1970s might have occupied a competitive position superior to its competitor firms, but generalized technological advancement ultimately posed a greater threat; the advent of the personal computer and the word processor eliminated much of the demand for typewriters. In this case, it was an environmental factor—technological advancement—and not a competitive factor that most dramatically impacted the firm. Similarly, a travel and tourism company might offer customers a superior value when compared to its direct competitors, but the firm's prospects might feel a more substantial impact resulting from larger economic trends. After all, a more competitively attractive tourism option for consumers may be insufficient to overcome the effects of an economic recession that eviscerates demand for travel and tourism overall. Once again, an environmental factor—in this case, macroeconomic conditions—exerts a significant impact on a firm's value proposition.

These are just two examples of factors in the broader societal environment that can dramatically impact the strategic outlook for a firm. They illustrate why it is important to consider such factors in assessing a firm's strategic position and competitive options.

Strategists should also pay attention to trends in the political and regulatory environment as such factors can also impact a firm's prospects in a substantial way. Government regulation and other forms of market intervention can directly affect a firm's operations and strategic options, and therefore should be carefully considered when formulating and implementing a firm's strategy.

In addition to technological, macroeconomic, and regulatory factors, a firm's context also includes many tacit influences that can arise from geographic differences, cultural trends, and social norms. These broad institutional factors constitute the "rules of the game" for doing business[iv] within that societal context and can influence a firm's actions. A firm is well advised to carefully study and understand the social forces that could influence its operations or the demand for its products or services. What's more, doing so may yield other important benefits; for example, a thorough environmental analysis might allow you to predict the behavior of a firm's competitors. Furthermore, an environmental analysis might illuminate opportunities to influence certain factors or rules of the game through direct engagement with relevant stakeholders.

In conducting a strategic analysis, a business strategist should be careful to not ignore the institutional forces in the broader social environment.

How do we use it?

Step 1. List factors.

The first step in an environmental analysis is to identify a set of factors of interest for the competitive setting. Most consulting firms (and strategy text books) have their own, sometimes proprietary frameworks, yet most contain roughly the same elements. A list of common factors of interest for an environmental analysis might include:

- **Demographic trends**: analysis of the current and changing population distribution of the consumer base within an industry.

- **Sociocultural influences**: analysis of features that influence consumers' choices including values, beliefs, and societal attitudes.

- **Technological developments**: analysis of new technologies and their potential impact on consumers' choices and competitive dynamics.

- **Macroeconomic impacts**: analysis of large-scale economic trends (inflation, exchange rates) and their impact on the industry.

- **Political-legal pressures**: analysis of relevant laws, regulations, and policies.

- **Global trade issues**: analysis of impacts of globalization and international governance bodies on industry competition.

Step 2. Collect data.

The second step is to collect data and information to help shed light on each of these factors. **Table 3-1** lists some of the specific considerations one may consider under each of these factors. Many but not all of these may be quantifiable.

Table 3-1. Potential considerations in environmental analysis.

DEMOGRAPHIC TRENDS	SOCIOCULTURAL INFLUENCES
• population growth and death rates • age distribution trends • migration/immigration • population segmentation	• lifestyle and fashion trends • social issues • media views and influence • ethnic/religious differences

MACROECONOMIC IMPACTS	POLITICAL-LEGAL PRESSURES
• influence of business cycle • home economy situation and trends • overseas economies and trends • taxation issues • seasonality of demand • market volatility due to wars/conflicts	• current and pending legislation • regulatory bodies and processes • environmental/social pressures • public funding for grants and initiatives • influence of lobbying/advocacy groups

TECHNOLOGICAL DEVELOPMENTS	GLOBAL TRADE ISSUES
• maturity of current technology • emergent technology developments • public and private research funding • technology licensing and patents • intellectual property legislation	• interest and exchange rates • international trade/monetary policies • international pressure groups • international legislation • globalization impacts

FOUNDATIONAL READINGS

Baron, D. "Private Politics, Corporate Social Responsibility, and Integrated Strategy." *Journal of Economics and Management Strategy* 10 (2001): 7–45.

Bourgeois, L. J. III, and Kathleen M. Eisenhardt. "Strategic Decision Processes in High Velocity Environments: Four Cases in the Microcomputer Industry." *Management Science* 34 (1988): 816–35.

North, D. *Institutions, Institutional Change, and Economic Performance*. New York: Cambridge University Press, 1990.

4. Five Forces Analysis

What is it?

Five forces analysis is a tool that enables managers to study the key factors in an industry environment that shape that nature of competition: (1) rivalry among current competitors, (2) threat of new entrants, (3) substitutes and complements, (4) power of suppliers, and (5) power of buyers.

When do we use it?

In a strategic analysis, five forces analysis is an excellent method to help you analyze how competitive forces shape an industry in order to adapt or influence the nature of competition. Collectively, the five forces determine the attractiveness of an industry, its profit potential, and the ease and attractiveness of mobility from one strategic position to another. Because of this, the analysis is useful when firms are making decisions about entry or exit from an industry as well as to identify major threats and opportunities in an industry.

Why do we use it?

This analysis was originally developed by Michael Porter, a Harvard professor and a noted authority on strategy. While all firms operate in a broad socioeconomic environment that includes legal, social, environmental, and economic factors, firms also operate in a more immediate competitive environment. The structure of this competitive environment determines both the overall attractiveness of an industry and helps identify opportunities to favorably position a firm within an industry.

Porter identified five primary forces that determine the competitive environment: (1) rivalry among current competitors, (2) threat of new entrants, (3) substitutes and complements, (4) power of suppliers, and (5) power of buyers. (See **Figure 4-1**.)

1. Rivalry. Among the direct and obvious forces in the industry, existing competitors must first deal with one another. When organizations compete for the same customers and try to win market share at the expense of others, all must react to and anticipate their competitors' actions.

2. Threat of entrants. New entrants into an industry compete with established companies placing downward pressure on prices and ultimately profits. In the last century, Japanese automobile manufacturers Toyota, Honda, and Nissan represented formidable new entrants to the U.S. market, threatening the market position of established U.S. players GM, Ford, and Chrysler. The existence of substantial barriers to entry helps protect the profit potential of existing firms and makes an industry more attractive.

3. Substitutes and complements. Besides firms that directly compete, other firms can affect industry dynamics by providing substitute products or services that are functionally similar (i.e., accomplishing the same goal) but technically different. The existence of substitutes threatens demand in the industry and puts downward pressure on prices and margins. While substitutes are a potential threat, a *complement* is a potential opportunity because customers buy more of a given product if they also demand more of the complementary product. For example, iTunes was established as an important complement to Apple's iPod, and now the firm has leveraged connections among its suite of products including iPhone, iPad, and the like.

4. Power of suppliers. Suppliers provide resources in the form of people, raw materials, components, information, and financing. Suppliers are important because they can dictate the nature of exchange and the potential value created farther up the chain toward buyers. Suppliers with greater power can negotiate better prices, squeezing the margins of downstream buyers.

5. Power of buyers. Buyers in an industry may include end consumers, but frequently the term refers to distributors, retailers, and other intermediaries. Like suppliers, buyers may have important bargaining powers that dictate the means of exchange in a transaction.

Figure 4-1. Five forces framework.

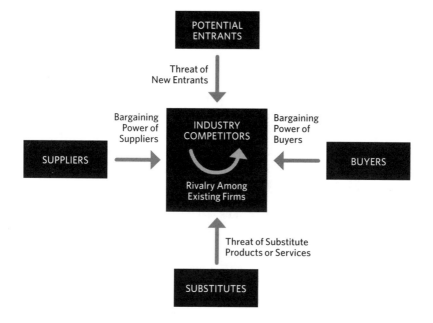

According to Porter, successful managers do more than simply react to this environment; they act in ways that actually shape or "enact" the organization's competitive environment. For example, a firm's introduction of substitute products or services can have a substantial influence over the competitive environment, and in turn this may have a direct impact on the attractiveness of an industry, its potential profitability, and competitive dynamics.

How do we use it?

Step 1. Analyze rivalry among existing competitors.

First identify the competitors within an industry. Competitors may include (1) small domestic firms, especially their entry into tiny, premium markets; (2) strong regional competitors; (3) big new domestic companies exploring new markets; (4) overseas firms, especially those that either try to solidify their position in small niches (a traditional Japanese tactic) or are able to draw on an inexpensive labor force on a large scale (as in China); and (5) newer entries, such as firms offering their products online. The growth in competition from other countries has been especially significant in recent years, with the worldwide reduction in international trade barriers.

Once competitors have been identified, the next step is to analyze the intensity of rivalry within the industry. One of the big considerations is simply the number of firms within an industry. *All else being equal, the more firms in an industry, the higher the rivalry.* It is tempting to look at duopolies—industries with two dominant players (e.g., Coke and Pepsi)—and declare they have "high rivalry." But duopolies are far less competitive—and typically far more profitable—than the alternative of many firms competing. Two additional considerations include whether (1) the incentives to "fight" are low and (2) coordination between competitors is possible. We consider each in turn.

Rivalry will be less intense if existing players have few incentives to engage in aggressive pricing behavior (i.e., slashing prices to gain market share). A number of things push back on this tendency. For example, substantial market growth within an industry, especially if firms are capacity constrained, lowers the incentive to fight. Similarly, if there are opportunities to differentiate offerings, firms can avoid head-to-head competition. The cyclical nature of demand in an industry can also be a big driver. Industries where demand ebbs and flows either with the business cycle or seasonally tend to suffer from overcapacity in the down times. During these times, firms have high incentives to cut prices in an attempt to use their excess capacity. Consider hotels in college towns: They tend to have huge demand on a limited number of weekends throughout the year (e.g., football games and graduation). As a result, they usually have excess capacity the rest of the year. Simply observe the prices at your average college town hotel on a random Tuesday in July. Prices will likely be substantially lower than during peak demand times.

Coordination that helps reduce pressures to engage in aggressive price cutting may be possible between competitors. In the extreme, firms may explicitly coordinate pricing and/or output. OPEC is a moderately successful cartel of oil-producing nations that tries to control the price of oil. In most mature economies, such explicit collusion is restricted as an antitrust violation. But there are sometimes factors that facilitate tacit coordination. For example, few competitors raise the prospects that firms will simply settle on a high price. This is more likely to occur in industries where there is a dominant player that others may follow. More homogeneity among competitors also raises the prospects for this to occur. Best-price clauses—matching the best price of your competitor—can also serve paradoxically as a way to keep prices higher by removing the benefits of slashing your own prices.

Step 2. Analyze threat of new entrants.

There are three main categories of considerations when assessing whether new entrants are likely to enter an industry. In particular, potential entrants are less likely to enter if:

1. Entrant faces high sunk costs. Sunk costs are investments that cannot be recovered once invested. While it is true that one should not consider sunk costs once invested ex ante (i.e., beforehand), the likelihood of investments being sunk increases the riskiness of an investment and thus raises the threshold for entering an industry. High capital expenditures, in and of themselves, do not pose a high barrier to entry. Arguably, if the future cash flows accruing to entrants are attractive, a firm should be able to raise capital from financial institutions. For example, R&D is a sunk cost that, if required to enter an industry, could raise risk and deter entry. On the flip side, a large multipurpose facility, while expensive, is less risky if it could be repurposed in the event of an exit from the industry (i.e., a large investment but one that is not sunk). In this case, this capital cost would be less of a barrier to entry.

2. Incumbents have a competitive advantage. If potential entrants are at a competitive disadvantage compared to existing players, it simply may not be profitable to enter. Examples of potential barriers to entry of this type include legal barriers such as patents and licenses. For example, the requirement that practicing lawyers must pass the bar exam creates a barrier to entry to the legal profession. Pioneering and iconic brands can also be a significant barrier to entry. In the soft drink industry, Coca-Cola and Pepsi have nearly unassailable positions due largely to their brands. Another barrier can be precommitment contracts, for example, that give access to distribution networks that lock in incumbent firms and lock out potential entrants. For example, in some regional markets, entry into the airline industry is difficult because existing players have locked up gate access at local airports. Finally, the presence of economies of scale and/or learning curves can thwart entry by potential new entrants. Economies of scale drive down costs for large, incumbent players, making it difficult for new entrants to be cost-competitive. Learning curves (e.g., the time and effort it takes to

develop a capability or technology) can also be a significant barrier to entry as new entrants struggle to catch up to existing firms.

3. Entrant faces retaliation. Entry is less likely if potential entrants may be forced out of business by the strategic, often pricing, behavior of incumbents. Such aggressive behavior must be credible, however. For example, if incumbents have excess capacity, they are incentivized to cut prices in the face of new entrants. They can do so because they can easily meet any increase in demand given their unused capacity. Another example is the presence of large exit costs. Exit costs are payments that must be made to shut down operations within an industry. These may include such things as obligations to health and retirement benefits programs or environmental liabilities for cleaning up a polluted facility. Exit costs create a barrier to entry by raising the prospects that existing players will "fight to the death" rather than exit the industry themselves. Ultimately, incumbents can create a reputation for aggressiveness (scaring away potential entrants). This reputation must be credible, however. Often this is difficult to establish unless the industry is dominated by a limited number of players. Otherwise, aggressiveness suffers from a free-rider problem where other incumbents do not respond in kind to the aggressiveness of one of their rivals.

Step 3: Analyze substitutes and complements

Technological advances and economic efficiencies are among the ways that firms can develop substitutes for existing products. The introduction of video game systems created a substitute for television viewing that has drawn a large share of young people out of TV audiences. Evidence suggests that young teens used their discretionary income to buy video games, thereby diminishing the market for music CDs. More recently, the makers of video games have said that Internet sites such as YouTube and Facebook have lured video game players away from their TV sets to interact with one another online.

In addition to the threat of current substitutes, companies need to think about potential substitutes that may be viable in the near future. For example, as alternatives to fossil fuels, experts suggest that nuclear fusion, solar power, and wind energy may prove useful one day. The advantages promised by each of these technologies are many: inexhaustible fuel supplies, electricity "too cheap to meter," zero emissions, universal public acceptance, and so on. Yet while they may look good on paper—and make us feel good about our choice—they often come up short in economic feasibility or technical viability.

The main thing to consider is the cross-price elasticity of a potential substitute. The cross-price elasticity is the percentage change in demand for one good given a 1% change in price for another good. For example, a 1% increase in the price of butter will likely lead to a large increase in demand for margarine. In this way, butter and margarine are elastic—they are significant substitutes and have high cross-price elasticity. Be aware that the cross-price elasticity among products may change over time. While cellular and landline phones historically did not substitute for one another, cellular is now a major competitive threat to traditional landline business.

A final consideration is whether there are substantial switching costs between products. A switching cost is the cost incurred to adopt an alternative product. In the case of butter and margarine, the switching costs are negligible if not zero. On the other hand, the switching cost for substituting car rental for public transportation is extremely high if you do not know how to drive an automobile.

Step 4. Analyze the power of suppliers.

Organizations are at a disadvantage if they become overly dependent on any powerful supplier. Suppliers are powerful if the firms in an industry have few other sources of supply or if suppliers have many other buyers (e.g., an oligopoly). Small numbers determine the extent of bargaining power. This power is increased by the existence of switching costs, in this case, fixed costs firms incur if they change suppliers. If, for example, a firm installs a supplier's equipment, such as computer software, it faces both economic and psychological costs in doing so.

On the other hand, firms in an industry have power if they have many alternative sources of supply or if they have a credible threat of integrating backward to provide their own sources of supply. Not surprisingly, supply chain management is particularly important in industries where the potential power of suppliers is high.

A final consideration is the availability of reliable information on suppliers. An industry benefits from having well-known information on supplier prices. The industry is further helped if suppliers cannot easily segment the market and thus struggle to price-discriminate.

Step 5. Analyze the power of buyers.

Once again, numbers help determine the extent of bargaining power. For example, when firms have only a small number of buyers (e.g., oligopsony), those buyers have more alternatives and may play competitors against one another, courting different offers and negotiating the best terms. In these cases, when buyers exert power, they can demand lower prices, higher quality, unique product specifications, or better service.

Switching costs play a role in this exchange as well. Distribution networks may provide advantages to firms, but when they cannot easily modify or change the nature of distribution, a firm may find an important barrier between itself and its end consumer.

Finally, information asymmetries matter as well. Unlike suppliers, however, less available information benefits the industry because they may leverage this information advantage to thwart attempts to play firms off one another and can potentially price-discriminate between buyers.

Step 6. Integrate and assess.

Taken together, five forces analysis provides a template that can help managers better characterize the industry environment. One of the key challenges to a five forces analysis is balancing between the various pressures, both positive and negative, on the industry. There is no simple way to balance these competing pressures. The strategic analyst must look at the totality of the forces and make an overall assessment of the industry's attractiveness.

Figure 4-2 depicts two analyses of industries representing extreme conditions. If managers do not understand how the environment affects their organizations or cannot identify opportunities and threats that are likely to be important, their ability to make strategic decisions that influence or adapt to competitive forces will be severely limited.

Figure 4-2. Examples of five forces analysis.

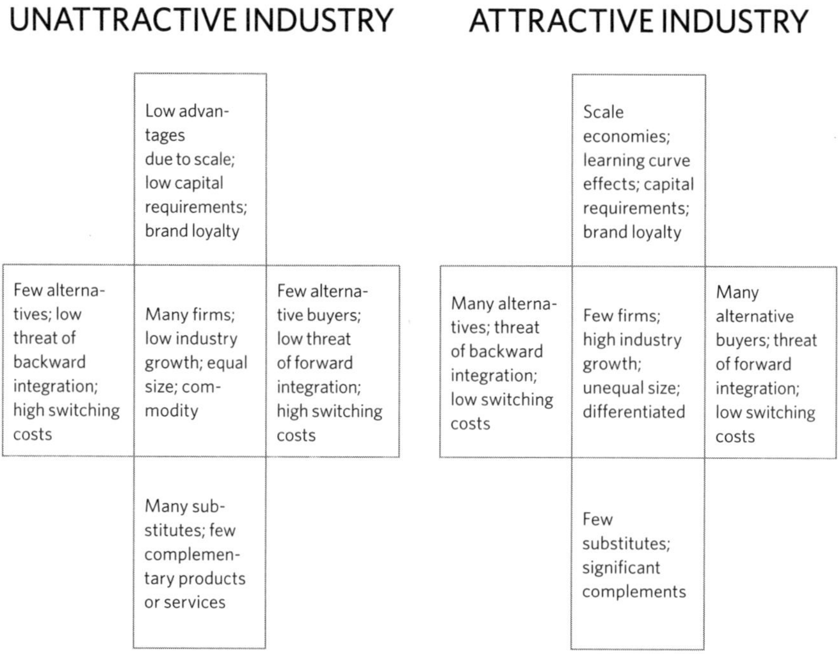

UNATTRACTIVE INDUSTRY

	Low advantages due to scale; low capital requirements; brand loyalty	
Few alternatives; low threat of backward integration; high switching costs	Many firms; low industry growth; equal size; commodity	Few alternative buyers; low threat of forward integration; high switching costs
	Many substitutes; few complementary products or services	

ATTRACTIVE INDUSTRY

	Scale economies; learning curve effects; capital requirements; brand loyalty	
Many alternatives; threat of backward integration; low switching costs	Few firms; high industry growth; unequal size; differentiated	Many alternative buyers; threat of forward integration; low switching costs
	Few substitutes; significant complements	

||||||||||||||||||||||||||||||||||||||||||||||||||||||||||||||||||||||||||

FOUNDATIONAL READINGS

Oster, Sharon. *Modern Competitive Analysis.* New York: Oxford University Press, 1999.

Porter, Michael. "The Five Competitive Forces That Shape Strategy." *Harvard Business Review* (January 2008).

5. Competitive Life Cycle Analysis

What is it?

Competitive life cycle (CLC) analysis is the assessment of competition within dynamic market environments.

When do we use it?

CLC analysis is used to evaluate the nature of competition as a market evolves. It can be used to help determine strategy in dynamic environments providing insights into the timing and positioning of new product introductions and other competitive options.

Why do we use it?

Scholars have long observed that technologies and product markets tend to progress along well-defined sigmoid or S-curves (**Figure 5-1**). Early in the history of a new technology or product concept, businesses experiment with new designs. Performance on various attributes of interest to customers such as quality or speed may be lacking. Adoption by consumers may be slow at first as some pioneering customers buy but others wait to see how the technology or product concept develops. Over time, performance improves. Growth in demand accelerates. New firms enter the market in an attempt to grab a piece of the action. A dominant design may emerge, resulting in most businesses providing similar offerings and features. Eventually, markets become saturated. Growth slows, and a shakeout among competitors occurs. The wait begins for the emergence of the next new thing that will replace the old technology, thereby jumpstarting a new S-curve, and the process begins all over again.

Figure 5-1. Industry S-curve.

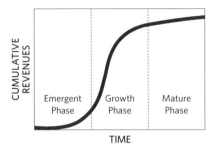

This is a natural aging process that cannot be reversed or avoided. An organization can only endeavor to create a portfolio of new initiatives that might produce a new product or service, to jump to a new S-curve, to replace the income lost upon the decline of existing products or services. One of the key roles of executives is to allocate resources in a manner that continuously produces new S-curves to replace declining ones keeping an organizational viable for a longer time. Growth results from scaling new products and services up the S-curve and also occurs from the continuous creation of new S-curves. So in one sense, the purpose of strategy is to create new S-curves. We know that not all growth forays or initiatives create new S-curves. This result can occur, for example, when new products do not meet customer needs or if customers do not perceive a good value or the competition can produce a similar product faster and cheaper.

Figure 5-2. The competitive life cycle.

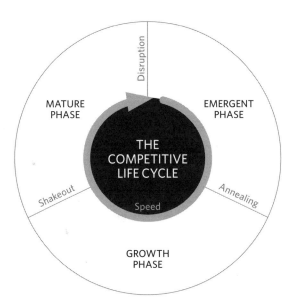

The CLC is split into three phases consistent with the S curve: an emergent phase, a growth phase, and a mature phase. Imagine the CLC is a racetrack (**Figure 5-2**). Each lap around the track represents a single S curve. While some firms may be in the mature phase of a technology or product concept, others may have moved to the next "lap" by introducing new technologies or products. The "race" continues as new generations of technologies and products compete over subsequent laps.

Demarking each of the three phases associated with a single S curve are transitory inflection points: disruption, annealing, and shakeout. The emergent phase begins with a *disruption*—the introduction of a new technology or product concept. Classic examples would be the introduction of horseless carriages (i.e., automobiles) into the vehicle market, the word processor into the typewriter market, and big-box store concepts in the retail sector. More recent examples include the advent of digital media players pioneered by Rio and others (and later Apple with the iPod) in the market for personal transportable music. These disruptions can vary quite dramatically in how disruptive they are to the competitive status quo. Some seemingly benign innovations can be quite radical to existing businesses. For example, the introduction of quartz watch technology in the 1960s led to a quick and devastating competitive reordering, with older Swiss watchmakers who specialized in mechanical (wind-up) watches being shoved aside by Japanese quartz watch manufacturers. Other disruptions may preserve and reinforce the dominance of existing businesses. Famously—or infamously—Microsoft was able to leverage its position in the operating system market and its expertise in software to capture the emerging market for browsers from the likes of Netscape.

After a disruption occurs, the new S-curve begins, and we enter the *emergent phase*. This period is often characterized by what others have referred to as the "era of ferment" as businesses experiment with various designs. In the early days of the automobile, in addition to gasoline-powered internal-combustion engines, there were steam-powered cars, electric vehicles, and automobiles powered by kerosene. During this phase, we typically observe widespread entry by both diversifying incumbent firms and new ventures. In some industries, the emergent phase can be shockingly brief. The evolution of social networking software occurred very quickly, with Facebook setting the standard and quickly overtaking rivals such as MySpace. In others, the emergent phase can last for decades. For example, hydrogen fuel cells have been around for decades, yet there is still no consensus on exactly what technological approach or design will work best. In part, what drives the length of this phase is the amount of effort put into advancing the technology or product. If businesses put more effort into a particular technology trajectory (e.g., spending more resources on R&D), they may shorten the emergent phase.

The emergent phase ends as customer adoption accelerates, and the product concept solidifies around a core set of design features. In many cases, what emerges is a dominant design—an often surprising similarity between product offerings. We refer to this process as *annealing*—a reduction in variance in product offerings. Witness the unfolding market for smartphones. The introduction of the iPhone by Apple seems to have accelerated the annealing process, leading Google and Microsoft to offer smartphones with similar product features and look and feel. Not all technologies or product concepts reach this transition. Some fail outright or linger in development for perpetuity. Laserdiscs, an early predecessor to the DVD, never gained traction in the media storage market.

Annealing typically gives way to the *growth* phase. As uncertainty in the technology or design is reduced, more customers are willing to purchase, leading to significant growth in demand. Business focus typically shifts from development to scaling. This is not to say that products and technologies do not continue to evolve and advance, but greater emphasis is placed on replication and expanding to meet growing demand. Firms continue to enter the market, many trying to catch the new wave of demand. Witness the flood of imitators of Starbucks once it pioneered the coffeehouse chain concept in the United States and began to expand. This phase is often characterized by increasing head-to-head competition, in many cases putting downward pressure on prices. "Complementary" capabilities in manufacturing, sales, and service begin to grow in importance relative to innovation and design.

As the growth phase winds down, when marginal growth rates begin declining, a competitive *shakeout* often ensues. Marginally competitive firms exit the market, and a handful of dominant players emerge. Shakeouts can vary in intensity. In the early U.S. automotive market, there were hundreds of competitors that through a series of bankruptcies and acquisitions were reduced to the Big Three: General Motors, Ford, and Chrysler. After Prohibition, hundreds of new breweries entered the U.S. beer market only to face consolidation and dominance by Anheuser-Busch, Miller, and Coors by the 1980s. The early digital music player market saw entry by the likes of Rio, Dell, HP, Microsoft, and Sony before becoming dominated by Apple. In some industries, dozens of large competitors may continue to compete after the shakeout. In others, the industry may be dominated by one or two players. In the extreme are winner-take-all markets that favor a single dominant player. See, for example, Microsoft's dominance of the PC operating system market or Google's dominance in online search technology.

After the shakeout, industries enter the *mature* phase. Growth is still possible, but it is likely to be less pronounced and often comes from stealing market share from competitors. When the market continues to support a number of rivals, competition can be particularly fierce with strong downward price pressure. Companies that thrive in the mature phase often focus on incremental innovation and cost savings. Total quality management and Six Sigma programs are common. We still may see entry of new firms in the mature phase, but new entrants tend to be small players capturing unexploited niches in the market. Some of these new entrants may even experience significant growth by, for example, pioneering low-cost approaches. In the PC industry, Acer has emerged as significant player, grabbing market share from the likes of Dell and HP. The mature phase can last decades or can be frustratingly short (at least to dominant players). The automotive industry has been relatively stable for decades with relative consistency in both the core technology and the set of competitors (with the exception of entry by some Asian producers). Now the automotive industry faces a potentially significant disruption with the introduction of hybrids and electric vehicles. The market for computer operating systems has been dominated by Microsoft, a relatively young firm, but that position is already threatened by the rise of mobile computing and smartphones.

The mature phase ends with the introduction of a new disruptive technology or product concept starting the entire process anew. We refer to the *speed* of the industry to characterize how long it takes to complete a cycle (i.e., a single lap). Once again, industries can vary dramatically in their speed. Much has been written of how globalization and information technology may be increasing the speed of all industries. People speak of "hyperdynamic" competition and the innovation imperative. Clearly, some industries are facing very fast cycles. For decades, the microprocessor industry has adhered to Moore's law that there is a doubling in processing capacity approximately every 18 months. The game player console industry has seen eight generations or cycles in the past 30 years.

In some cases, it is important to recognize that a competitive life cycle may be nested or "fractal." Fractal is a term borrowed from complexity theory that is used to characterize the property of systems that show self-similarity when broken into smaller units. It may be useful to think of the competitive life cycle over long and short time periods. While the auto industry has been relatively stable and suggests a long life cycle, there have been individual component technologies (e.g., electronics, safety features) that it may be useful to think of as having their own life cycles.

How do we use it?

Step 1. Charting your positions on the CLC.

In order for a business to make appropriate strategic decisions, management must have a good picture of the timing and projected life of its existing products over the CLC. The first step in analyzing the CLC is to chart existing income streams delineating the position of each product. The positioning of your current products determines how much time you have left before you must replace that income. The amount of time will influence your investment strategy, especially the decision to develop new products or to buy new products that have been successfully developed and commercialized but not scaled by you or others. The positioning will also determine the allocation of investments among technology-enabled development, commercialization, scaling, and improvements; in essence, the composition of your growth portfolio.

Unfortunately, many firms find it difficult to explore new growth when they are intoxicated by scaling growth with existing products. This intoxication blurs the reality that at some point this too will pass, and the star product's popularity will decline. If a product is a big generator of net profit upon its decline, then management often has to resort to a big investment in either a new product or an acquisition because it did not invest previously to generate a portfolio of initiatives that could produce new S-curves. Not all initiatives will produce new S-curves. In fact, most new initiatives do not produce new S-curves, which is why management—in anticipation of the decline of current S-curves—must create a portfolio of initiatives to hedge its bets. Charting your positions should give you better information about the projected life cycle of your current revenue streams. This will allow you to chart your growth needs: the amount of revenue you have to replace plus the amount of revenue you need to add to maintain your growth and satisfy your stakeholders.

See **Figure 5-3** for a stylized map for Apple, circa June 2011. Let's start with Apple's Macintosh PC. Given current demand for PCs, this market appears to be well in the mature phase. Apple has a relatively small position (about 6% market share) in a highly competitive, fragmented market. The emergence of mobile computing (e.g., smartphones and tablets) may very well signal the end of this segment in the not too distant future. The iPad and similar tablets may, in fact, represent the next lap in this race. Tablets have been around for decades (starting with Apple's Newton in the early 1990s) but only now seem to be transitioning now to the growth phase. The market is characterized by significant number of entrants, though much of this is annealing around the iPad design. This looks to transition to the growth phase over the next few years (and Apple has already experienced significant penetration with the iPad). The iPhone has benefited from a similar position in the smartphone market—the market leader setting the dominant design—and is in the growth phase of this market. One would expect a shakeout to be coming in smartphones soon. Finally, the iPod and portable digital players arguably have entered the mature phase. Growth rates are declining. A number of prominent entrants have left the market. How long this mature phase is likely to last is an interesting and important question for Apple.

Figure 5-3. Sample CLC: Apple, circa 2011.

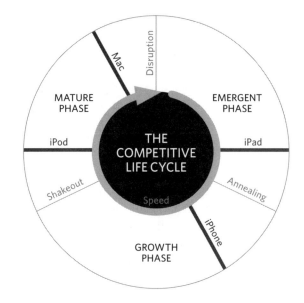

Step 2. Characterizing the CLCs for your businesses.

The next step in a CLC analysis is to characterize the specific competitive contexts where you compete. To aid in characterizing your businesses, consider **Table 5-1.** What is your forecast for the timing and severity of the transitory inflection points? Defining these will in turn specify the length and character of each phase of your S-curve (emergence, growth, and maturity). One can retrospectively identify these transitions by looking at market demand and entry and exit rates of firms. Looking at past epochs may give you a good sense of how future S-curves may play out. For example, graphing cumulative industry revenues for a product or technology class can produce an S-curve that can highlight transitions: Accelerated growth in revenues suggests transition to the growth phase, declining growth rates suggest a transition to the mature phase. Looking at entry and exit rates can help identify phase transitions: heavy exit rates with lower rates of entry suggest a shakeout is occurring and that the industry is transitioning to a mature phase. These indicators can help you understand how long each phase is likely to last and gauge the overall speed of the industry.

Table 5-1. Competitive life cycle worksheet.

PHASE	TIMING	SEVERITY
Disruption	How long is mature phase?	Radical, incremental, or architectural?
Annealing	How long is emergent phase?	Dominant design or multiple designs?
Shakeout	How long is growth phase?	Winner-take-all, duopoly, contested?
Overall	Slow burn or hyperdynamic?	

One can graphically represent differences in timing on the competitive life cycle by changing the relative size of one phase versus another. In some industries, emergence may be short relative to growth and maturity. Others may experience long periods of growth relative to the other two phases. Overall speed can simply be indicated as a scale on the map. For example, speed in the game player console industry is approximately four years. In microprocessors, speed equals 18 months. We can use this metric to characterize the overall industry. Is this a hyperdynamic environment or more of a slow burn? Is innovating new S-curves a matter of life and death or can we worry about this once we are well into the mature phase of the cycle?

Assessing severity is also important. Severity helps forecast how the competitive game is likely to play out. First, how severe are disruptions in the industry? Are they likely radical—fundamentally altering the underlying technology or business model rendering existing capabilities useless? Or are they more incremental—building on existing capabilities? Or are they perhaps architectural in nature—preserving core technologies but disrupting the way components or services are integrated or organized? More radical and architectural disruptions open the door for new entrants to come in and dominant the market. Second, how severe is the annealing likely to be? Do we expect a single dominant design to emerge or will there be space for multiple, fairly divergent offerings in the marketplace? For example, is there reason to believe that the marketplace will force standardization? Standardization will likely lead to increased competition, while less severe annealing may allow for multiple, differentiated players. Third, how severe is the shakeout likely to be? How many firms are likely to be left standing at the end of this life cycle? Is this a winner-take-all market? Will the mature phase support entry by smaller niche players? A winner-take-all market suggests placing great effort in capturing the market early, while more contested competitive environments may suggest emphasizing manufacturing and quality to outcompete firms in the mature phase.

Step 3. Assessing your competitors' positions.

Charting your current products on the competitive life cycle gives you a picture of your current reality. To put it in the context of your competitive environment, you need to chart as best you can your main competitors as well—realizing that new, unforeseen competitors may emerge. Who are the competitors in each market that you currently have positions in? What are their revenues and market shares? How long have they been in the market? Are they recent entrants or have they been competing in this segment for a while? Who is planning to enter this segment or is a likely entrant in the future?

Charting your competitors requires competitive research and an understanding of your competitors' investments and growth initiatives. Having a picture of your competitors' current product portfolios as well as the number and kind of investments being made to replace existing S-curves allows you to role-play and scenario-plan potential moves by each competitor. This type of analysis should help you evaluate which of your investment alternatives could produce a relatively competitive advantage for a period of time versus these competitors.

||||||||||||||||||||||||||||||||||||||||||||||||||||||||||||||||||||||||||||||

FOUNDATIONAL READINGS

Anderson, P., and M. L. Tushman. "Technological Discontinuities and Dominant Designs: A Cyclical Model of Technological Change." *Administrative Science Quarterly* 35 (1990): 604–33.

Christensen, Clayton. *The Innovator's Dilemma: When New Technologies Cause Great Firms to Fail.* Boston: Harvard Business School Press, 1997.

Hill, CWL. "Establishing a Standard: Competitive Strategy and Technological Standards in Winner-Take-All Industries." *Academy of Management Executive* 11 (1997): 7–25.

Makadok, R. "Can First-Mover and Early-Mover Advantages Be Sustained in an Industry With Low Barriers to Entry/Imitation?" *Strategic Management Journal* 19 (1998): 683–96.

McGahan, A. "How Industries Change," *Harvard Business Review* (October 2004).

Nelson, R. R., and S. G. Winter. A*n Evolutionary Theory of Economic Change.* Cambridge, MA: Harvard University Press, 1982.

Schumpeter, J. A. "The Theory of Economic Development." Cambridge, MA: Harvard Economic Studies, 1934.

Tushman, M. L., and P. Anderson. "Technological Discontinuities and Organizational Environments." *Administrative Science Quarterly* 31 (1986): 439–65.

PART 2.

Tools for Analyzing Competitive Position

6. Stakeholder Analysis[v]

What is it?

Stakeholder analysis is a framework for understanding the key individuals, groups, or organizations that can significantly affect (or be affected by) the activities of the firm. A focus on stakeholder interests clarifies what kind of value each stakeholder is looking for.

When do we use it?

A useful framework for understanding the many demands placed on a firm, a stakeholder analysis can be helpful for thinking about the firm's key relationships and interdependencies. Stakeholder analysis is, by nature, only one component of a more full strategic analysis. While a stakeholder analysis can highlight areas of potentially conflicting interests among stakeholders, it also highlights opportunities for the alignment of stakeholder interests. For instance, while employees, stockholders, and suppliers may all be looking for different kinds of value (measured in different ways), the insightful strategist looks for connections among these interests and works to align them.

Why do we use it?

Strategy is ultimately about how key constituencies such as customers, suppliers, employees, investors, and other stakeholders interact in order to create value. The executive's or manager's job is to understand and manage these relationships, and a successful firm is one that is effective at managing stakeholder relationships and interests.

Commercial firms can be understood as a set of relationships among these groups, all of which have a stake in the company's activities. The success of a business firm is enabled by the willing contributions of its key stakeholders, and all parties stand to benefit from the firm's success and have something to lose if the firm is mismanaged or fails altogether.

This points to a related insight from the stakeholder view of strategy: it is ultimately untenable to create value for one stakeholder by shortchanging another. Although such an approach might initially reward one stakeholder over others, this approach is impossible to sustain and will ultimately backfire. For instance, a firm might dramatically cut back its expenses by eliminating the customer service function of the organization, which would certainly reduce operating costs and therefore increase returns to investors—but eventually the poor customer service is likely to drive customers away, reduce revenue, and therefore diminish the firm's profits. An action intended to boost investor returns by shortchanging other key stakeholders, in other words, is likely to leave investors ill-served in the end.

How do we do it?

Step 1. Identify stakeholders.

First, it is important to simply understand who a firm's key stakeholders are. Oftentimes, this is accomplished by creating a stakeholder map (**Figure 6-1**). A basic stakeholder map simply starts with the firm and identifies who the primary and secondary stakeholders actually are. Primary stakeholders are vital to the continued growth and prosperity of the business; take away the support of any of these groups, and the business will likely be unable to sustain any sort of long-term competitive advantage. Secondary stakeholders, while perhaps not having a vitally important stake in the business itself, can nevertheless affect the relationship between the firm and its primary stakeholders.

Figure 6-1. Stakeholder map.

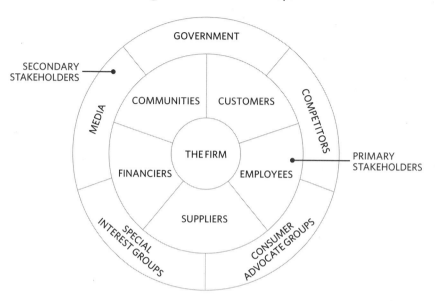

Step 2. Analyze stakeholder interests.

Once the primary and secondary stakeholders have been identified, it is often helpful to better understand the interests of those stakeholders. A better understanding of stakeholder interests facilitates better management of those interests and therefore improves the prospects for the firm's long-term success. Creating a stakeholder issues matrix is a way to begin to understand the positions of each stakeholder on key issues. This can be done in a simple spreadsheet as shown in **Figure 6-2**:

Figure 6-2. Example of stakeholder priorities for a hypothetical firm.

ISSUE	EMPLOYEES	CUSTOMERS	GOVERNMENT	COMMUNITY	SHAREHOLDERS
Product Safety	3	1	1	1	3
Job Fulfillment	1	5	5	3	5
Financial Returns	3	5	5	5	1
Impact on Environment	3	3	1	1	5

1 = Critical importance to stakeholder; **3** = Somewhat important to stakeholder; **5** = Not very important to stakeholder

Step 3. Assess impacts of strategic actions.

The final step in a stakeholder analysis is to examine the impact of a particular strategic action on the firm's various stakeholders (**Figure 6-3**). One could consider various strategic alternatives under consideration, and the potential impact (positive or negative, and how so) on the firm's stakeholders.'

Figure 6-3. Impact of stakeholder actions.

POTENTIAL ACTION	EMPLOYEES	CUSTOMERS	GOVERNMENT	COMMUNITY	SHAREHOLDERS
Alternative #1	?	?	?	?	?
Alternative #3	?	?	?	?	?
Alternative #3	?	?	?	?	?
Alternative #4	?	?	?	?	?

This not only facilitates the "weighing out" of different stakeholder interests in the various alternatives being considered but also can pave the way to innovative ways to align the interests of various stakeholders, or at the very least, improve some of the tradeoffs among them.

|||||||||||||||||||||||||||||||||||||||||||||||||||||||||||||||||||||||||||||||||||||||

FOUNDATIONAL READINGS

Chen, Ming-Jer, Gregory Fairchild, R. Edward Freeman, Jared Harris, and S. Venkataraman. "Creating Value for Stakeholders" UVA-S-0169 (Charlottesville, VA: Darden Business Publishing, 2009).

Donaldson, Thomas, and Lee E. Preston. "The Stakeholder Theory of the Corporation: Concepts, Evidence, and Implications." *Academy of Management Review* (1995).

Freeman, Edward R., Jeffrey Harrison, and Andrew Wicks. *Managing for Stakeholders*. Yale University Press, 2007.

Freeman, R. E., Jeffery S. Harrison, Andrew C. Wicks, Bidhan L. Parmar, Simone de Colle. *Stakeholder Theory: The State of the Art*. New York: Cambridge University Press, 2010.

Freeman, R. E. *Strategic Management: A Stakeholder Approach*. Boston: Pittman, 1984 (reprinted by Cambridge U Press 2010).

Friedman, A. L., and S. Miles. *Stakeholders: Theory and Practice*. New York: Oxford University Press, 2006.

Phillips, Robert. *Stakeholder Theory and Organizational Ethics*. San Francisco: Berrett-Koehler Publishers, 2003.

Phillips, Robert. *Stakeholder Theory: Impact and Prospects*. Northampton: Edward Elgar Publishers, 2011.

Phillips, Robert., and R. Edward Freeman. *Stakeholders*. Northampton: Edward Elgar Publishers, 2010.

Porter, M. E., and M. R. Kramer. "Strategy and Society: The Link between Competitive Advantage and Corporate Social Responsibility." *Harvard Business Review* 84 (2006): 78–92. Capabilities Analysis

7. Capabilities Analysis

What is it?

Capabilities analysis helps clarify the major sets of activities, skills, and resources that drive value to customers.

When do we use it?

Capabilities analysis can be useful at the time of strategy formulation—when firms are assessing which strategic options are currently feasible—and may be included in a broader process of determining strengths, weaknesses, opportunities, and threats (SWOT). In addition, capabilities assessment can be used as an initial step in strategy implementation. Assuming an appropriate time horizon, firms may use the analysis to ascertain which capabilities need to be enhanced or developed in order to execute a chosen strategy. As part of this, capabilities analysis can be used to determine which capabilities are perhaps noncore and therefore candidates for outsourcing or external partnering.

Why do we use it?

Truly understanding a firm's competitive strengths requires more than just an understanding of that organization's *tangible* assets. Indeed, the key building blocks of competitive advantage are often more likely to involve the firm's *intangible* assets. Such assets can be understood as the resources that organizations tap in order to create value, such as a tacit understanding of a complicated market segment, trusting relationships with key suppliers or customers, or an efficient set of back-end processes that produce faster or more responsive products.

Yet an intangible source of competitive success is not always by definition a capability. For instance, the innovativeness of a key product offering may indeed generate customer revenue and even capture sales that might have otherwise gone to a competitor. But what if that particular product was a fluke? Or what happens when that product no longer seems so innovative to customers? If a firm truly intends to compete on innovation, a more lasting source of competitive advantage may be the firm's *capability* around innovation, better understood as the intangible and tacit elements that enable the firm to innovate in the first place.

Successful companies are often those that develop strategies that align such capabilities with their plans for external positioning in the marketplace. Brilliantly formulated strategies mean little if the firm has not developed the capacity to execute them. In this sense, capabilities place an upper limit on which strategies are viable.

Capabilities analysis is based on the resource-based view (RBV) of strategy that emphasizes the internal skills and resources of the firm. The RBV asserts that resources and capabilities can be a source of competitive advantage when they are (a) valuable, (b) rare, (c) inimitable, and (d) nonsubstitutable. Valuable capabilities must be rare, otherwise they would hardly be a source of differentiation. Valuable, rare capabilities must be difficult to imitate, otherwise any competitive advantage would be exceedingly fleeting. And the most enviable capabilities are ones for which there are no readily identifiable substitutes. More generally, we can think of capabilities analysis as helping firms identify the specific ways in which they create value for their stakeholders and differentiate themselves from competitors.

How do we use it?

Step 1. Determine the value chain for your business.

First, draw the value network for the business being analyzed. This involves laying out the cluster of activities that creates value for a product or service, working backward from the end point of the value proposition delivered to customers. These clusters, taken together, form the basic architecture of the chain. It is important to note that a firm rarely participates in every cluster; it will outsource, relying on suppliers or distributors. A typical value chain might look like that in **Figure 7-1**:

Figure 7-1. Value chain.

Note: this model is perhaps artificially linear; these activities do not always occur in a single stream, nor are they always done in the same order each time.

An important—and often tricky—task is defining what constitutes an element in the network. Remember that we are mapping strategic clusters of activities, not companies. For a first pass, it is always better to make a more detailed map. You can later collapse clusters of activities that do not need to be viewed separately. If you start out too broadly, you may miss important activities that are invisible at too aggregated a level but could be broken apart to create strategic advantage.

Next analyze the competitive environment in each box, identifying the key players and their relative market shares. Identify the core strategic capabilities needed to produce value in each box. What does each contribute to overall value? Evaluate the bargaining power and influence of each player. Who drives performance? How easy would it be to find a substitute for each player's con-tribution? How much value does the end customer perceive as contributed by this player? Determine the possibilities for improving a firm's power and profitability in the network. What determines how value is captured? Who has the power in the network? Why? Assess a firm's vulnerabilities. Where is a firm vulnerable to others who might change its footprint in ways that put it at a disadvantage? Identify themes related to bargaining power, capabilities, partners, and defensibility.

Step 2. Isolate the core set of capabilities.

Now identify the clusters of activity where a focal firm has core capabilities that are central to its competitive success. In reality, not every activity in a value chain is likely to be a core capability. Most firms recognize that there is a small set of three to six capabilities that are most critical to customer value creation and that may differentiate them from competitors. Other activities may only be "table stakes" necessary to play but insufficient to win competitively. The question is where is the organization world-class?

Capabilities are more than just the activities described in the value chain. They are combinations of three key knowledge-based resources: (a) processes, (b) people, and (c) systems (technologies) that drive value. In this regard, capabilities represent the collective learning in organizations and involve how the firm coordinates diverse skills and integrates multiple technologies.

> **Step 2a. Processes.** Processes are an important foundation of core capabilities because they represent codified knowledge, recipes, or standard routines for how work will be done and the results will be accomplished. In this step, identify those processes that are most critical to the capability.
>
> This will likely not include every process but rather those few that are most pivotal. For example, when executives at Intermountain Healthcare (IHC) analyzed its capability in clinical care, they found that less than 10% of its processes accounted for over 90% of the cost, time, and quality of patient health. These were selected as the core processes on which the organization would focus for capability enhancement. Similarly, during Lou Gerstner's early years at IBM, he focused on six core processes as the foundation for the company's strategic repositioning (hardware development, software development, supply chain, services, fulfillment, and customer relationship management). The company viewed these as most visible to customers and therefore most critical to capability development.
>
> **Step 2b. People.** Human capital is perhaps the most obvious source of knowledge-based advantage. In this step, it is important to identify the key skill areas that are most critical for executing and improving the processes above. Again, not everyone who touches a process is strategic. Critical talent might include process owners, and/or those

with the biggest impact on three process metrics: (a) cycle time, (b) quality or defects, and (c) cost.

Typically, we can identify critical skill areas as those that are (a) most central to value creation and (b) unique and difficult to replace. Importantly, skill level and pay are not always the best indicators of strategic talent in this context. Southwest's capability in ground operations depends less on the skill of its pilots (who are justifiability well paid), and more on the skill of its ramp agents and operations agents, who turn the planes around and get them back in the air. Note this is also not a search for the best performers. "Racking and stacking" the best performers is an important but separate activity from identifying key skill areas. In this step, the analysis is meant to identify the A positions rather than the A players.

Step 2c. Systems. In addition to core processes and talent, knowledge-based resources are also codified in supporting systems and technologies. This may include information systems, databases, proprietary technologies, and the like. These systems have three primary impacts: (a) operational, (b) relational, and (c) transformational. First, some systems have an operational impact in that they help to automate processes, improve efficiency, and reduce/eliminate human effort. Second, these systems have a relational impact, helping to connect people to one another or to important databases. Increasing these systems helps to "infomate" work by providing information that enables higher quality and more timely decision support. Finally, systems have a transformational impact in that they may actually change the sequence or pattern of work. In fact, there are times when the systems are virtually indistinguishable from the processes.

Step 3. Determine degree of alignment.

The next step in the analysis is to determine if the people, processes, and systems are aligned (i.e., internal alignment) and also aligned with the customer value proposition (i.e., external alignment).

Step 3a. Internal alignment. Firms often note that they have made improvements in some elements of capability development but have neglected others. For example, executives in a professional services firm recently lamented that although the firm had invested heavily in process improvement and skill development to enable knowledge sharing among its more than 20 global offices; it had not made concomitant investments in information systems to enable knowledge transfer. Instead the systems were designed to ensure timely reporting to top management. As a consequence, despite good intentions and a culture of collaboration, the consultants could not leverage solutions to problems in one part of the world that had been developed in another. As a result of poor internal alignment, the firm's capability in global knowledge management was far behind its goals.

Step 3b. External alignment. What is driving a customer's willingness to buy from your firm? What benefits do they derive relative to the costs that they incur (i.e., value = benefits/costs)? Generic value propositions might include some combination of product leadership (e.g., Apple, Lexus), operational excellence (e.g., FedEx, Southwest), and customer intimacy (e.g., Nordstrom, McKinsey). These value propositions provide focus for an organization's strategy and could be a source of differentiation. Are capabilities aligned with the customer value proposition? This seems like an obvious question, but when properly aligned the impact of even simple and straightforward capabilities can be substantial. In contrast, misalignment can be devastating.

A simple example is in the story of Domino's Pizza. Most observers would agree that Tom Monahan, founder of Domino's, was able to change the pizza industry, not because he created a better product, but because he was able offer a different value proposition—30 minutes or it's free—and then created the capability to deliver against that promise. He aligned the key people, processes, and systems necessary to develop a capability in home-delivery pizza. Domino's used assembly-line-based standardized processes to improve efficiency and reduce preparation time. It was the first to use conveyor-belt oven technology to ensure uniform temperature and reduce baking time, and it incentivized delivery personnel to get the pizza to homes within 30 minutes.

As important as what Domino's did is what it did *not* do. Strategy is about making choices. Domino's did not focus on great pizza—it focused on fast pizza. It did not customize every order but prepared all orders in advance. It didn't hire premier pizza chefs who tossed pizza dough up in the air to make lighter crusts. It didn't use wood-fired stoves to give the pizza an old-world taste. And it didn't offer in-store dining. These would add cost and time that customers did not want. Each ingredient in Monahan's formula was aligned with its value proposition of fast delivery.

It might be interesting to note that, although other start-ups were able to copy Monahan's strategy, its major competitor—Pizza Hut—could not. Although Pizza Hut tried home-delivery pizza, its efforts failed miserably. Its capabilities were misaligned with that value proposition. Pizza Hut's capability, its people, processes, and systems, were aligned with a different value proposition of in-store dining and quality pizza.

Step 4. Determine sustainability.

The final step of a capabilities analysis is to determine the sustainability of distinctive core capabilities. The competitive advantage that accrues with certain capabilities may be undermined by two general forces:

Step 4a. Imitation. Core capabilities provide a competitive advantage only to the extent that others cannot imitate them. A number of factors may limit the imitability of core capabilities. Scarcity is one. A dining experience augmented by a prime location (e.g., on a dock by the sea) may be difficult for others to replicate due to limited real estate opportunities. Capabilities derived from socially complex, integrative sets of activities may be difficult to imitate (e.g., the theme park experience at Disneyland). Ambiguity about the underlying process or source behind a capability may hinder imitation by others. The key question is: Can others imitate a given capability and how long will it take?

Step 4b. Durability. Even a difficult-to-imitate capability may fail to continue to provide value if the underlying basis for that capability degrades over time. An obvious example is intellectual property such as a patent that only provides legal protection for a fixed number of years (typically 17 years in the United States). Human capital, to the extent that it is embodied in an individual or individuals, will eventually degrade. Consider a championship-level sports team. As its star players age, performance will eventually decline. Most assets such as property and equipment degrade over time. The key question is: How long can we maintain a given capability, imitation aside?

For each core capability identified, assess the degree to which it is difficult to imitate and the durability of the capability. This will help you plan for how long you might enjoy a competitive advantage but also help highlight when investment might be needed to move onto other capabilities or to refresh existing capabilities.

Taken together, these steps in a capabilities analysis provide a concrete way to assess an amorphous element of strategic analysis. Intangible assets, such as capabilities, can be powerful sources of advantage. Their amorphous nature makes them difficult to copy, but they can be nearly impossible to manage if firms do not have a method by which to make some elements tangible.

Figure 7-2 provides a template for making the analysis more explicit:

Figure 7-2. Capability worksheet.

CAPABILITIES	1. _____	2. _____	3. _____	4. _____
Processes	• • •	• • •	• • •	• • •
People (Skills)	• • •	• • •	• • •	• • •
Systems/ Tech	• • • •	• • • •	• • • •	• • • •
Alignment & Sustainability	• • •	• • •	• • •	• • •

|||||||||||||||||||||||||||||||||||||||||||||||||||||||||||||||||||||||||||

FOUNDATIONAL READINGS

Barney, J. "Firm Resources and Sustained Competitive Advantage." *Journal of Management* 17 (1991): 99–120.

Collis D., and C. Montgomery. "Competing on Resources." *Harvard Business Review* 73, no. 4 (1995): 118–28.

Dierickx, Ingemar, and Karel Cool. "Asset Stock Accumulation and Sustainability of Competitive Advantage." *Management Science* 35, no. 12 (December 1989): 1504–511.

Eisenhardt, Kathleen M., and Jeffrey A. Martin. (2000) "Dynamic Capabilities: What Are They?" *Strategic Management Journal* 21, no. 10 (October/November 2000): 1105–121.

Leinwand, Paul, and Cesare Mainardi. "The Coherence Premium." *Harvard Business Review* (June 2010).

Morris, Shad S., and Snell, Scott A. (2011) "Intellectual capital configurations and organizational capability: An empirical examination of human resource subunits in the multinational enterprise" *Journal of International Business Studies,* vol. 42, 805–827.

Teece, D. J., G. Pisano, and A. Shuen. "Dynamic Capabilities and Strategic Management." *Strategic Management Journal* 18, (1997): 509–33.

Wernerfelt, Birger. "A Resource-Based View of the Firm." *Strategic Management Journal* 5, no. 2 (April–June 1984): 171–80.

Wernerfelt, Birger, (2013) "Small forces and large firms: Foundations of the RBV" *Strategic Management Journal,* vol. 34, Issue 6, 635–643.

8. Strategy Maps

What are they?

A strategy map, often referred to as a "perceptual map" in marketing, is a tool for visually displaying the position of a company or a line of business relative to competitors. Strategy maps generally place firms based on two or three dimensions that capture either critical elements driving consumer preferences or important attributes characterizing competition.

When do we use them?

Strategy maps are widely used in strategic analyses and may be part of a broader competitor or industry analysis. In marketing, strategy maps are frequently used to highlight differences in consumers' perceptions across various product lines. Strategy maps are particularly useful for understanding and illustrating a company's competitive position relative to rivals and to identify the generic strategies of firms (e.g., whether a firm is a low-cost competitor, a differentiated player, or a niche player within an industry).

Why do we use them?

Strategy maps are useful visual tools to quickly communicate a large amount of information on a collection of firms. These flexible tools are fairly easy to generate and can appear in a number of different formats and for a number of different uses. One of the primary uses in a strategic analysis is to identify the generic strategies of firms (see matrix that follows). Arguably, there are four main ways a firm can position itself within a market, defined by the source of competitive advantage a firm pursues and the firm's competitive scope within an industry (**Figure 8-1**).

Figure 8-1. Generic strategies.

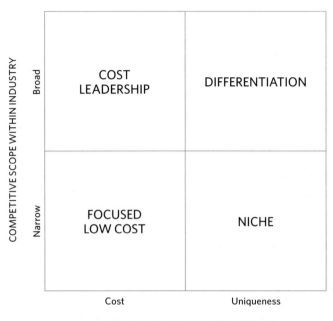

SOURCE OF COMPETITIVE ADVANTAGE

In general, there are two types of competitive advantage a firm can pursue: low cost or uniqueness. Using a low-cost strategy, a firm simply tries to have lower costs than the marginal producer in the industry. The marginal producer is the firm that is just viable in the marketplace—generating revenues at roughly its opportunity cost. With the uniqueness strategy, a firm tries to persuade customers to pay more. A uniqueness strategy usually entails offering products of higher quality or with more features than other products in the marketplace.

Firms may choose to target a broader or narrower segment of the market. Most markets can be segmented into smaller product markets defined by geography, buyer characteristics (e.g., age, race, income, and gender), and other product line characteristics. Broad-scope firms tend to deliver products and services that appeal to a wide number of these segments. They may do so by offering individual products and services with broad appeal or by offering a portfolio of products that cover the product space. For example, Henry Ford's Model T automobile was built with a broad target market in mind: people who wanted a simple, affordable car. Alternatively, General Mills offers a broad array of cereals to try to appeal to each market segment. Both are examples of broad-scope strategies. On the opposite end of the spectrum are narrow strategies that target one or a few market segments. Porsche manufactures and sells high-end sports cars to a narrow segment of affluent automobile owners. Nature's Path Organic sells healthy cereals to a narrower, environmentally and socially conscious consumer base.

These two dimensions, broad versus narrow and low cost versus unique, define four generic strategies:

1. Broad-scope, low-cost players are referred to as cost *leaders.* Wal-Mart is a classic example of a company trying to appeal to a wide audience with the lowest-cost products. Others include Dell Computers, Mc-Donald's Restaurants, and Nucor Steel. Cost leaders typically engage in aggressive cost-cutting, build market share to gain economies of scale, use low-cost inputs and labor, minimize overhead such as R&D, and invest in low-cost, state-of-the-art operations and continuous improvement initiatives.

2. Broad-scope, unique players are referred to as *differentiated players.* The Target Corporation is illustrative of this strategy. A mass-market retailer, it offers higher-quality products in a more refined setting (and at higher prices) than Wal-Mart does. Other examples include Apple, Intel, and Goldman Sachs. Differentiators often invest heavily in advertising to build brand awareness, develop innovative capabilities to stay on the cutting edge, and invest heavily in human resources and other ancillary activities.

3. On the narrow side, we have both *focused, low-cost players* and *differentiated niche players.* Kia entered the U.S. market as a focused, low-cost auto manufacturer—offering a narrow line of low-cost cars to a limited market. On the flip side, Tesla was a new entry into the U.S. automobile market with an electric-powered sports car—a higher-end vehicle costing over $100K and appealing to a narrow set of environmentalists and technophiles (not to mention celebrities). In both cases, these firms tried to deter rivalry by narrowly dividing the market. They might gain expertise and knowledge through their focus. In the case of niche players, their focus may increase their brand loyalty and allow them to achieve status with a prestige product.

4. Some firms pursue generic strategies that cross these boundaries. Toyota is a classic example of a company that has simultaneously attempted to be both low cost and high quality (i.e., unique). Southwest Airlines is another company that has successfully pursued a low-cost strategy while also differentiating itself in terms of service. Michael Porter and others argue that firms do so at their own risk, however. Rare is the firm that can successfully pursue low cost and differentiation at the same time. More often than not, these firms get stuck in the middle—being neither the lowest-cost player or all that differentiated in the market.

How do we do it?

Step 1. Select dimensions.

The first step in generating a strategy map is to determine the dimensions. Dimensions can be any factors that help define competition within an industry. These may be based on product styling, such as the conservative versus the sporty automobiles or luxury versus mass-market leather goods. They may be based on price. In other words, low versus high, or they may be based on capabilities or technologies common in the industry, such as microbrews versus mass-produced beer or minimills versus integrated steel mills. Dimensions that capture basic competitive indicators may be used (e.g., revenues, market share, or earnings).

Step 2. Assess dimensions.

The second step is to assess a firm or one of its product lines on each dimension. In the best case, this can be done quantitatively. For example, price is a dimension that is relatively straightforward to map. Other dimensions might require customer surveys or expert opinions to quantify and map as when customer perceptions on quality or customers' loyalty ratings are needed. As a last resort, the analyst may elect to assess firms and businesses based on their intuition or knowledge of the industry.

Step 3. Create map.

The final step is to place firms on the map based on these assessments. Creating two-dimensional maps is straightforward. You can create three-dimensional maps by using circles to represent the third dimension—the larger the circle, the greater the value on that dimension. The template below gives an example of a three-dimensional map of the auto industry. The two main dimensions for analysis are the degree to which a car model is conservative versus sporty and the quality of the vehicle as measured by defects. The third dimension is represented by the size of the circle and captures the revenues for each car model (**Figure 8-2**).

Figure 8-2. Example of a strategy map.

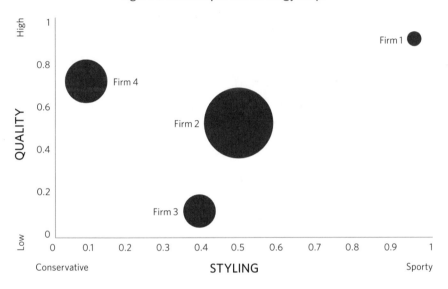

This map conveys some valuable information. For example, you can identify the competitive position of the various firms and their apparent strategy. Firm 1 is relatively small and has positioned itself to sell high-quality, sporty vehicles— a classic niche strategy. Firm 2 is the market leader selling large numbers of vehicles to a presumably broad audience. Firm 3 seems to be pursuing a low-cost strategy, selling vehicles of average quality. Firm 4 may be pursuing a differentiated strategy, perhaps targeting an older consumer base and selling higher-quality vehicles with conservative styling.

||||||||||||||||||||||||||||||||||||||||||||||||||||||||||||||||||||||||||||||||||||

FOUNDATIONAL READINGS

Grant, R. *Contemporary Strategy Analysis*. Oxford: Blackwell Publishers, 2008: Chapters 8 and 9.

Dess, Gregory G and Peter S. Davis. 1984. Porter's (1980) Generic Strategies as Determinants of Strategic Group Membership and Organizational Performance. *Academy of Management Journal,* 27(3): 467-488

Mintzberg, Henry. 1988. Generic Strategies: toward a comprehensive framework. *Advances in Strategic Management* 5(1): 1-67.

Deephouse, David. 1999. To be different, or to be the same? It's a question (and theory) of strategic balance. *Strategic Management Journal* 20(2): 147-166.

Robert S. Kaplan and David P. Norton. 2001. The strategy-focused organization: How Balanced Scorecard Companies Thrive in the New Business Environment. *Harvard Business Press.*

9. Portfolio Planning Matrices

What are they?

A portfolio planning matrix is a tool used to map businesses within a firm according to their current and potential ability to create value, along with their cash needs and other resource requirements. This facilitates budget allocation as well as diversification and acquisition decisions. Portfolio planning matrices first appeared in the 1970s as strategy consulting firms such as Boston Consulting Group (BCG) and McKinsey pioneered their use.

When do we use them?

As strategists' tools, diversification matrices can be useful starting points for thinking about the appropriate scope of firms and analyzing the relative value of firms' portfolios of businesses. They are limited, however, because they do not explicitly consider capabilities at the corporate level or the value that may be created through interactions among business units. Thus, portfolio planning matrices are by nature only a component of a deeper strategic analysis that must employ additional tools.

Why do we use them?

Firms often seek to leverage their position across different market segments and industries, using different product lines, service offerings, and other approaches to segment customers and create value. While each particular business unit or product line can and should pursue its own strategy for value creation, overall corporate strategy considers the strategies of various businesses in an integrated way. Corporate strategy highlights such questions as: When does a firm benefit from vertical integration? When is product diversification advisable? How can entry into a new market strengthen our position in existing markets? Ultimately, what is the correct portfolio of businesses for the firm to be in?

There are a number of reasons a firm may benefit from operating across multiple businesses. Historically, financial arguments have been advanced to justify large conglomerates of unrelated businesses. For example, it has been suggested that firms can use the retained earnings from one business to invest in other profitable opportunities. Furthermore, advocates of corporate diversification argue that firms can use a portfolio of business positions to lower volatility, hedge against risk, and potentially lower their cost of capital; however, by and large, these claims have found little systematic support, and as a result, the arguments in favor of general corporate diversification have fallen out of favor. Not only is this lack of enthusiasm for corporate diversification driven by the evidence, it also makes sense. There is no reason to believe, for instance, that firms can make such investments any better than capital markets can, and there are some reasons to believe they are far worse. For example, such arguments have been used by executives in the past to build large empires with seemingly little efficiency or benefit to the organization's stakeholders.

That said, diversification can sometimes create value. But how? More acceptable reasons for diversification are the potential for operational and strategic benefits. Operational benefits include capturing economies of scale and scope through multiple business positions and being able to leverage capabilities across businesses. Honda in particular has been very successful in leveraging its capability in small-engine design and manufacturing to compete in such diverse sectors as cars, motorcycles, lawn equipment, and personal watercraft. In the simplest cases, multiple positions can allow a firm to share common functions and resources, eliminating duplicate effort and lowering costs.

In addition, potential strategic benefits include (1) eliminating and preventing competition by subsidizing a price war, (2) reducing rivalry through mutual forbearance, and (3) raising rivals' costs through vertical foreclosure. In the first case, firms can leverage their position across multiple markets to compete aggressively in other segments. Microsoft's dominant position in PC operating systems makes it a tough competitor in other segments such as browser software. In the second case, if firms compete across multiple markets, it actually may have the effect of lowering rivalry. This is the concept of "mutually assured destruction," an idea that was commonly asserted during the Cold War. If one firm behaves aggressively in one market, that aggression may lead to retaliation in many other markets. This threat lowers the likelihood that firms will be aggressive in the first place. The final element, vertical foreclosure, applies most often in cases of vertical integration where a firm tries to cut off a rival by moving upstream into supply. Barnes & Noble infamously tried to do this by acquiring Ingram Books, the dominant wholesaler in the industry, in an attempt to cut off Amazon.com's supply chain.

How do we do it?

We begin with the classic portfolio planning matrix devised by BCG. BCG's growth-share matrix groups a firm's businesses into four broad categories based on combinations of market growth and market share relative to the largest competitor. Once the firm's businesses are mapped, BCG provides the following guidance: Low market share businesses in mature industries are "dogs" and should be divested. High market share businesses in mature low-growth markets are "cash cows" that generate more cash than they consume and should thus be milked (i.e., held but not necessarily invested in). High market share businesses in growing industries are "stars" and should definitely be held and may become future cash cows. "Question marks" could become either dogs or cash cows as the industry matures.

The BCG matrix (**Figure 9-1**) has come under much criticism over the years, especially with regard to the prescriptions recommended for each quadrant. It is not always the case that the firm with the largest market share is, in fact, a profitable firm. Similarly, not all growing markets are attractive, especially if the industry lacks barriers to entry or other barriers to competition.

Figure 9-1. The BCG matrix.

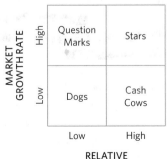

A related portfolio planning matrix, originally pioneered by McKinsey and General Electric, addresses some of these issues. The McKinsey/GE approach (**Figure 9-2**) puts industry attractiveness on one axis and business unit competitive advantage on the other allowing the criteria to expand beyond market growth and market share. Industry attractiveness includes future industry demand prospects but also includes industry structure. Competitive advantage focuses on the possession of resources and capabilities that allow a firm to outperform rivals regardless of their market share. McKinsey recommends that firms invest in businesses where they have a competitive advantage and the industry is attractive, divest (or "harvest") business units where competitive advantage is low and the industry unattractive, and hold (or "milk") businesses on the off-diagonals.

Figure 9-2. The McKinsey matrix.

MCKINSEY MATRIX

	Low	High
High	Hold	Build
Low	Harvest	Hold

INDUSTRY ATTRACTIVENESS (vertical axis, High / Low)

BUSINESS UNIT COMPETITIVE ADVANTAGE (horizontal axis, Low / High)

But at best, such matrices can only serve as general rules, and such prescriptions are certainly not ironclad. And both approaches suffer from essentially viewing the individual businesses in isolation from one another, missing a key mechanism for corporate value creation. At the end of the day, the portfolio of businesses a firm retains should be based on the value they create by being co-owned. To put it another way, the whole should be greater than the sum of the parts. How does the holding of one business help a firm's competitiveness in another business? In some cases, a firm may be willing to accept losses in one business (sometimes called a "loss leader") if it aids another.

Diversification and consolidation decisions are important strategic decisions; firms often pursue diversification to create economies of scope (e.g., product scope, geographic scope) or to realize economies of internalizing transactions. But diversification decisions must be made carefully, as each of these potential advantages has another side. Can too much diversification engender a lack of focus? What are the costs associated with internalization and vertical integration?

||||||||||||||||||||||||||||||||||||||||||||||||||||||||||||||||||||||||||||||||

FOUNDATIONAL READINGS

Collis, David, and Cynthia Montgomery. "Creating Corporate Advantage." *Harvard Business Review* (May 1998).

Prahalad, C. K., and R. A. Bettis. "The Dominant Logic: A New Linkage between Diversity and Performance." *Strategic Management Journal* 7, no. 6 (1986): 485–501.

Rumelt, R. "Diversification Strategy and Profitability." *Strategic Management Journal* 3, no. 4 (1982): 359–69.

PART 3.

Tools for Analyzing
Strategic Decisions

10. Hypothesis Testing

What is it?

Hypothesis testing is a method for unearthing the key assumptions about what must be true about a strategic choice; it then seeks data to assess the likelihood that these assumptions are true.

When do we use it?

Hypothesis testing can be used to assess any strategic choice faced by a firm or analyst. It is a critical component of analyzing whether to pursue a particular course of action: whether to enter a new market, to invest in a research project, or to acquire another firm.

Why do we use it?

Every strategic choice is a *hypothesis*—a proposition that a particular action will cause a determined outcome. The conditions and assumptions the hypothesis rests on must be valid in order for it to be true. And so testing these assumptions is essential.

Assumptions must be clearly articulated before they can be tested. We have only two options for testing them: (1) use existing secondary data to conduct an analytical *thought* experiment or (2) go out into the field and gather new data. Since finding new data tends to be costly and visible, we try to conduct early tests using data we already have.

When strategies fail, it is *always* because reality turns out to be different than we thought it would be: perhaps customers don't want a new offering, a firm can't execute it, partners don't like it, or competitors copy it quickly. Hypothesis testing focuses on identifying the make or break elements of a strategic choice. It involves taking a cold hard look at its key vulnerabilities.

How do we use it?

Step 1. Identify core assumptions.

To get started, first drill down to the core assumptions on which the success of a proposed strategic action depends. In general, a common set of tests applies to just about any strategic decision:

1. The value test. If executed well, the strategic action will create value. For example, a new product offering will be desired by customers at a price that works.

2. The execution test. The firm can create and deliver the strategic action at a cost that works.

3. The scale test. The strategic action can be sustained and leveraged to create future value that makes it worthwhile.

4. The defensibility test. Competitors can't easily copy the strategic action.

Imagine that you are a newly appointed business development officer at a home loan company recently acquired by a large credit card firm, and you have been given a mandate to identify and develop a new growth opportunity. Your new parent company is one of the largest credit card issuers in the United States with more than 60 million accounts worldwide and a reputation as a leader in direct marketing and online services. Besides credit cards, it offers a variety of financial services such as auto loans, small business loans, home equity loans, and second mortgages. It does not, however, offer first mortgages. Being new to the mortgage business, for several months, you immerse yourself in the ins and outs of the mortgage industry and finally identify a number of what you believe to be high-potential growth opportunities. One of your favorite ideas is for a first mortgage product aimed at high-net-worth customers of the parent company, delivered with personal service through your bank branches. You believe that your proposed concept can pass all four of these tests:

1. Customers will value the convenience of personal attention from your bankers, one-stop shopping for all their financial needs, and the superior rates your knowledge of their credit history will allow you to offer them.

2. Your parent company's capability to deliver outstanding quality and fast turnaround time online for financial products is well known; you also have a set of bankers available already in your branches.

3. Historical data tell you that your parent organization has 35 million customers with excellent credit ratings; thus the future potential business opportunity is substantial.

4. Established competitors in the marketplace, such as Bank of America and Wells Fargo, are presently distracted by cleaning up the mess in their subprime mortgage business, and you see an opportunity to enter without fear of retaliation on their part.

These are the foundation of your core assumptions for your hypothesis that the new mortgage product is worth pursuing. Make sure your assumptions relating to each individual test (value, execution, defensibility, and scalability) are as explicit as you can make them. Lay out *specific* tests that your hypothesis must pass in order to move forward. These tests relate to your firm and your particular situation.

Continuing with our example, recognize that these key assumptions revolve around a set of educated guesses you've made about:

Customers. Specify why this concept will create superior value for customers beyond existing options, how much they will be willing to pay, and whether there are enough of them to constitute a market of sufficient size. In our example, as you think more deeply about your embedded assumptions, you realize that your value proposition rests on a number of important assumptions: one being that your high-net-worth customers value the face-to-face service delivered by your bankers.

Your Organization. How will the organization create and deliver the promised value, and what current capabilities will the organization leverage? You must also identify which critical capabilities are missing and whom you will partner with to obtain these. For example, while your parent organization's superb online capability set is well established, your ability to deliver this new product also rests on the skill of your branch bankers. Do they have the necessary skill set, you wonder? You also realize that you are assuming that your parent's scale in its Internet-driven credit card business will apply to scaling a personal service business.

Competitors. Which competitors are likely to be affected and how will they react? This would include assumptions about whether and why they are capable of copying the strategy quickly and how else they might interfere with your ability to succeed. Though competitors in the field are numerous, you are assuming that they will not notice or retaliate against your entry into their market.

Determine which assumptions are most critical to the potential attractiveness of your proposed strategy. If you've been thorough, you have probably generated far more assumptions than you can feasibly test. Can you highlight the handful of assumptions that make or break your new idea? Timing is also important to consider. Generally, the two tests that matter most in the early stages of a new idea are the value and execution tests. Scaling and defensibility come later as you know more. Most new strategies fail the former (value test) rather than the latter (execution test). Referring to our example, you may decide that the value test is the place to start. If a significant proportion of your target high-net-worth customers do not value either the personal service you intend to provide or the convenience of one-stop shopping, your concept is unlikely to succeed.

Step 2. Conduct thought experiments.

Next identify the data that would allow you to conclusively test the key assumptions. Having narrowed the assumptions down to a manageable number, you now begin to move from unearthing assumptions to testing them. It is crucial here to think through what the data that would either confirm or disprove your hypotheses about the attractiveness of the new strategy would look like. Here you are identifying the information you *need* and then figuring out how to get it.

Sort the data you need into one of the following three categories: what you know, what you don't know and can't, and what you don't know but could. Let's look at each category in turn:

What you know. These are the facts that you already have in your possession related to each assumption. Beware of beliefs masquerading as facts. Don't confuse the two. The doubters will help you with this by highlighting the areas where your personal (and sometimes optimistic) interpretations may be blinding you to some realities that need to be acknowledged. In our example, you know quite a bit. For instance, you know that your parent company has a great capability set for doing financial transactions online and that it has a lot of high-net-worth customers already.

What you don't know and can't know. This is the stuff that you can't know without a crystal ball. It is the land of true uncertainty—the land of the unknowable. No number of experiments—either thought or real—can resolve this uncertainty. The only thing you can do here is predict. For example, there are some macro issues that matter to your new concept's success—issues such as housing starts and prime rate levels. You could make some predictions here, but you aren't sure how to really test these except against "expert" opinions.

What you don't know but could. In any situation, there is a lot of stuff that is knowable—but you haven't yet taken the time to go and get the data to know it yet. Generally, this can be an expensive proposition, and you don't want to chase data you don't need. That is why it is so critical to be hypothesis-driven in your approach: identifying only the really important data and then expending the effort to go get it. Some of these data may already exist elsewhere, and you just need to go out and collect it. This is why consulting firms flourish—this is what they do. Going back to our example: As you reflect upon it, you realize that there are a lot of customers out there who you could identify, already in the parent's database, whose views about issues such as convenience and personal service you could better understand. There is also probably some information on the kind of qualifications the bankers in your branches have floating around somewhere, maybe in HR.

The data in category #3 (what you don't know but could) lends itself to thought experiments. Identify what it would take to get the data quickly. You are going to have to construct some data, which means not relying on what your internal accounting systems or industry trade group—or whomever—decides to give you. In our example, you decide that determining how your target customers feel about personal service and value does not lend itself to a thought experiment. After all, they are already there in the database, you know who they are, and they are reasonably inexpensive to reach. Why conduct a lot of analyses based on past data that may not be reflective of what they really think, when you can easily just ask some of them?

Design your thought experiment paying special attention to the data that could prove you wrong. Go collect data and begin to validate or invalidate the core assumptions underlying your assumptions.

‖‖‖

FOUNDATIONAL READINGS

Brown, T. "Design Thinking." *Harvard Business Review* (June 2008).

Liedtka, Jeanne, and Tim Ogilvie. *Designing for Growth.* New York: Columbia Business School Publishing, 2011.

Martin, R. *The Opposable Mind: Winning Through Integrative Thinking.* Boston: Harvard Business School Press, 2007.

Martin, R. *The Design of Business: Why Design Thinking Is the Next Competitive Advantage.* Boston: Harvard Business School Press, 2009.

11. Payoff Matrices

What are they?

Payoff matrices are visual representations of the payoffs associated with the strategic moves of a focal player given the moves and countermoves of competitors. Though typically depicted as a 2×2 matrix where two players are contemplating two strategic decisions, more complicated payoff matrices with multiple players and numerous decisions can be constructed.

When do we use them?

Payoff matrices, and game theory in general, are well suited for the analysis of a discrete number of options among a limited number of competitors. Duopoly situations (i.e., where two firms are competing directly) are the easiest types of games to analyze (e.g., Coke and Pepsi in soft drinks or Boeing and Airbus in large aircraft manufacturing). Payoff matrices can be used to analyze a wide variety of strategic decisions such as pricing (price high or low?), product design (high quality or low quality?), mergers and acquisitions (acquire or don't acquire?), research and development (invest or don't invest?), and entry (enter market or not?).

Why do we use them?

Payoff matrices are a common way to represent simple competitive games and are a staple of game theoretic analysis. Game theory is the formal analysis of conflict and cooperation among intelligent and rational agents. A branch of mathematics, it has found widespread application in economics and, in particular, the study of competitive strategy. Payoff matrices are often used to identify dominant strategies—those that are optimal, regardless of what a competitor does.

How do we use them?

Step 1. Identify strategic actions available to competitors.

The first step in creating and analyzing a payoff matrix is identifying the competitors and the choices that you wish to analyze. Consider this matrix representing a pricing decision between Coke and Pepsi. Here we have a simple 2 × 2 game where our two competitors are considering one of two strategic actions: price high or price low (**Figure 11-1**).

Figure 11-1. Coke/Pepsi pricing decision.

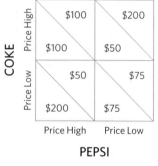

Payoffs represent revenues in $M

Step 2. Assess the value associated with each strategic action contingent on competitors.

To complete the table, collect data on the payoffs associated with each strategic option. A formal analysis of future discounted cash flows resulting from an option may be in order. This is often a challenging exercise because data on future contingencies may not be readily available. You may be forced to make educated guesses. A thorough sensitivity analysis of the payoffs may be in order when analyzing the game.

Referring again to our Coke versus Pepsi matrix, we present the payoffs, in this case revenues in $millions, to Coke in the lower-left triangle of each cell of the matrix and the payoffs to Pepsi in the upper-right triangle of each cell. For example, if both price low (lower-right quadrant), they will split demand and enjoy revenues of $100 million each. If both price high (upper-left quadrant), they will split demand, and while overall demand will be lower, the higher price will lead to revenues of $100 million each. If Coke chooses to price high and Pepsi chooses to price low (the upper-right quadrant), Pepsi will capture more demand and therefore collect more revenues despite the lower price. Similarly, if Pepsi chooses to price high and Coke chooses to price low (the lower-left quadrant), Coke will capture more demand and collect more revenues. In this way, the matrix in our example is a symmetric game—the payoffs to Coke and Pepsi are the same for each combination of strategic choices. Games needn't be symmetric, and the analysis of asymmetric games remains the same.

Step 3. Identify dominant strategies.

The final step in creating and analyzing a payoff matrix is to look for dominant strategies. A dominant strategy, once again, is a strategy that is optimal, regardless of what a competitor does. To illustrate, consider Coke versus Pepsi again; if Coke prices high and Pepsi prices low, Coke would be foolish not to slash prices in response. To do so would increase Coke's payoff from $50 million to $75 million. While Pepsi and Coke would both prefer to price high (payoff = $100 million each), neither is willing to do so without a guarantee that the other would follow suit. Even if both choose to initially price high, each is incentivized to slash prices, doubling its payout from $100 million to $200 million. Thus, the likely outcome is both Coke and Pepsi will slash prices (i.e., choose the low price option).

This scenario is a common game referred to as the "prisoner's dilemma." In the classic case from which it got its name, two suspects (or prisoners) are being interrogated by police in separate rooms. The best outcome is for both to reveal nothing and thus avoid going to jail; however, each is at risk of the other placing the blame on the other and thus facing significant jail time. The police further incentivize each suspect to turn on their partners in crime by offering the possibility of a plea bargain if one places the blame on the other. As a result, both end up confessing and going to jail.

While the prisoner's dilemma game is helpful in explaining why it is difficult for firms to tacitly collude to hold prices higher, the fact is that many competitive interactions avoid this fate. Consider the asymmetric diversification decision illustrated below. In this case, to diversify is a dominant strategy for Firm 1 regardless of what Firm 2 chooses (i.e., to diversify always means its payoff is higher). Knowing this, Firm 2 will choose to not diversify because it knows Firm 1 will diversify (i.e., the payoff is higher for not diversifying given that Firm 1 will diversify). (**See Figure 11-2.**)

Figure 11-2. Example of a diversification decision.

Payoffs represent revenues in $M

Note that simple payoff matrices represent competitive interactions as single-period simultaneous games. In other words, the players make their strategic decisions at the same time rather than sequentially, and they only play the game once rather than repeatedly. Imagine how the game above would be different if played sequentially. Who goes first would make a big difference in the outcome. To represent a sequential game, you can convert a payoff table into a decision tree (**Figure 11-3**). A decision tree is a visual representation of the strategic moves and countermoves of players in a sequence. See the illustration. To analyze a decision tree, look forward and reason back. Consider the decision tree on the top: if Firm 1 diversifies, Firm 2 will choose not to diversify. If Firm 1 does not diversify, Firm 2 will. Knowing that, Firm 1 will diversify as that gives it the greatest payoff. Now flip it around.

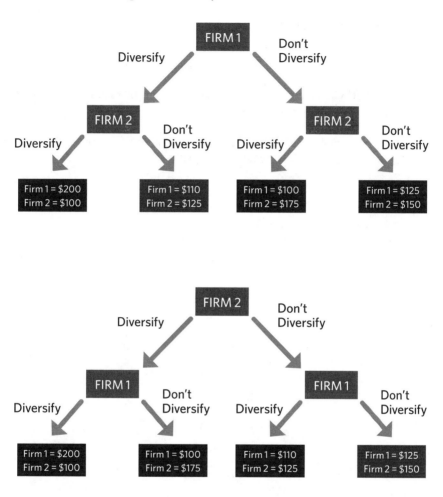

Figure 11-3. Example of a decision tree.

In the tree on the bottom, if Firm 2 goes first, the optimal outcome is "don't diversify" in which case Firm 1 will also not diversify. By going first, Firm 2 is able to force Firm 1 into a decision more favorable to Firm 2.

In summary, payoff matrices in particular (and game theory in general) are a useful tool to understand the give and take of competitive dynamics as rivals fight for advantageous competitive positions.

||||||||||||||||||||||||||||||||||||||||||||||||||||||||||||||||||||||||||||||

FOUNDATIONAL READINGS

Chen, Ming-Jer. "Competitor Analysis and Interfirm Rivalry: Toward a Theoretical Integration." *Academy of Management Review* 21 (1996): 100–34.

Coyne, Kevin, and John Horn. "Predicting Your Competitor's Reaction." *Harvard Business Review* (April 2009).

Dixit, Avinas, and Barry Nalebuff. "Anticipating Your Rivals' Response." *Thinking Strategically*: New York: W.W. Norton, 1991.

12. Real Options Analysis

What is it?

Real options analysis is the assessment of strategic investments where a firm has the right, but not the obligation, to continue the investment at a later date.

When do we use it?

Real options analysis can be used to value any strategic investment where investment can be staged. It has found useful application in investments that involve innovative outputs such as new product development and research and development projects.

Why do we use it?

Many strategic decisions unfold over time. While some strategic decisions require large up-front investments (e.g., acquisitions), many provide opportunities at a later date to either discontinue or to reinvest (e.g., alliances). One of the most obvious examples is investment in research and development projects. Typically, such investments can be staged so that progress can be reviewed and decisions can be made on whether to continue. In the biotech industry, new drugs move through a series of well-defined stages as they progress from concept to the marketplace shelf. At each stage, the firm can decide whether to discontinue the development effort or to invest further. Such investments are *real options* for future strategic actions to the extent they involve tangible assets as opposed to financial instruments.

A real options analysis is often contrasted with discounted cash flows (DCF) and net present value (NPV) approaches to project valuation and decision making. Unlike DCF and NPV, which require a single forecast of future cash flows, real options analysis allows for the valuing of flexibility—the ability to change course as an investment unfolds. This flexibility helps reduce risk because firms can terminate investments if information gathered is unfavorable, thereby avoiding further costs. As a result, projects that are characterized by flexibility and volatility are often valued higher using a real options valuation than DCF or NPV.

Real options analysis is not without its critics. Generally, two classes of criticism have been advanced. First, the data needed to conduct a thorough real options analysis is difficult to collect or estimate. Second, the applicability of real options analysis is limited to a fairly narrow set of strategic options. With that said, real options analysis can be a valuable tool in the *Strategist's Toolkit* for some investment decisions. Investments are rarely one-time commitments to a particular strategic course. Strategic analysts are constantly reassessing the prospects of a firm based on new data and events. Real options analysis highlights that value in strategic actions that leave future strategic options available. While a full-blown real options valuation may not be feasible in many situations, there is a great value in real options thinking as a way to structure strategic decision problems.

How do we use it?

The instructions below are a simple introduction to real options analysis. For a deeper treatment of the topic, please refer to the readings listed at the end of this chapter.

Step 1. Map out options.

The first stage in a real options analysis is to map out the decision tree for the investment under consideration. The decision tree in **Figure 12-1** illustrates the general logic of real options on a simple two-stage investment. A firm pursues a specific investment option in stage one: for example, a product development opportunity. It learns more about the potential of this course of action as data is generated in the development process. If the news is unfavorable, the firm may abandon this course of action, writing off the initial investment. If the news is favorable, it may make follow-on investments capturing value from its actions by commercializing the product.

Figure 12-1. Decision tree for a simple two-stage investment.

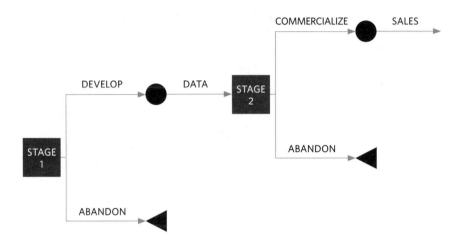

Step 2. Estimate model parameters.

After mapping out the options, you will need to estimate a number of parameters: the project value(s), the exercise price for each option, the option cost for each option, the time to option expiration, the volatility, and the risk-free interest rate. For each terminal path in the decision tree, calculate the *project value*—the NPV for each choice where an option is exercised. In the simple example above, this would be the NPV of the estimated stream of cash flows that would result from commercializing the product in stage 2. In other words, this is the expected cash flow if all goes well. Next calculate the *exercise price*—the cost of executing the option to commercialize the new product (e.g., the fixed costs of building a manufacturing plant or executing a marketing rollout). Do not conflate the exercise price and the project value. The *option cost* is the cost of purchasing the option. In our simple example, this is the cost of conducting research and development in stage 1. The *time to expiration* is the expected time from initial development to when cash flows from commercialization are received. The final parameters needed are the *volatility* and *risk-free interest rate* for investments in this sector.

Step 3. Compute option value.

With our parameter values estimated, we can price the option using a formal option valuation model, such as Black-Scholes. It is critical to consider whether the underlying distributional assumptions of the option valuation model adopted apply to the case at hand. For example, the Black-Scholes model assumes that the project value follows a lognormal distribution with a constant level of volatility. It is beyond the scope of this toolkit to provide instruction on specific option valuation techniques. We refer you to standard finance textbooks such as Brealey and Myers, *Principles of Corporate Finance* (McGraw-Hill) for detailed treatment of this topic.

With the option value in hand, we can compare it to the option cost and make an informed decision of the value of flexibility in decision making. Because it is often difficult to calculate reliable and specific estimates of the model parameters, sensitivity analysis is absolutely critical. Consider multiple estimates for the project value and other parameters. Real options analysis is merely an additional input into a thorough and thoughtful consideration of a strategic option.

||||||||||||||||||||||||||||||||||||||||||||||||||||||||||||||||||||||||||||||||||

FOUNDATIONAL READINGS

Adner, R. and D. Levinthal. "What Is Not a Real Option: Considering Boundaries for the Application of Real Options to Business Strategy." *Academy of Management Review* 29, no. 1 (2004): 74–85.

Bowman, E. H., and G. T. Moskowitz. "Real Options Analysis and Strategic Decision Making." *Organization Science* 12, no. 16 (2001): 772–77.

Folta, T. "Governance and Uncertainty: The Trade-Off between Administrative Control and Commitment." *Strategic Management Journal* 19 (1998): 1007–028.

McGrath, R. "Falling Forward: Real Options Reasoning and Entrepreneurial Failure." *Academy of Management Review* 24, no. 1 (1999): 13–30

Miller, K. D., and J. Reuer. "Asymmetric Corporate Exposures to Foreign Exchange Rate Changes." *Strategic Management Journal* 19, no. 12 (1998): 1183–191.

Williamson, P. J. "Strategy as Options on the Future." *Sloan Management Review* (Spring 1999).

13. Acquisition Analysis

What is it?

Acquisition analysis is the evaluation of the strategic value to one firm in acquiring or merging with another firm.

When do we use it?

Acquisition analysis is critical when considering a specific acquisition opportunity or analyzing a pool of potential acquisition targets. It can also be used as part of a broader analysis of the tradeoffs among various strategic options available to a firm including internal development, alliances, and partnerships in addition to acquisitions.

Why do we use it?

Mergers and acquisitions are some of the most significant strategic actions in which a firm can engage. Technically, an acquisition is a transaction where one firm buys another firm and integrates the acquired firm into its portfolio of businesses. A merger is a transaction where two firms agree to integrate their operations, creating a new legal entity. Some would argue that all mergers are ultimately acquisitions—that one party will effectively assume control of the new entity.

The frequency and importance of acquisitions tends to ebb and flow over time. Over the last 100 years, there have been five major waves of acquisition activity in the United States. In the past decade, there has been some substantial acquisition activity both domestically and globally across a wide number of sectors and involving trillions of dollars transacted in total. The attraction to acquisitions is obvious. They can be used to reduce competition, to diversify into otherwise hard-to-enter businesses, to quickly enter new attractive markets, and to acquire intangible assets and capabilities that would be difficult to build on one's own.

Acquisitions also require significant and unique capital budgeting decisions that are difficult to unwind once consummated. Managing integration of transacted parties can be extremely complex. Hoped-for synergies can be difficult to realize. Expensive acquisitions can cause a firm to become highly leveraged, thus reducing future strategic options. By some estimates, acquisitions reduce the value of the acquiring firm *on average* (see Sirower, *The Synergy Trap,* 1997). In other words, most acquisitions could be deemed failures.

Complicating matters is that firms frequently overpay for acquisition targets. Almost all acquisitions involve a premium paid over the existing valuation of a firm. In some cases, this premium can be 20% or more over the current market valuation of a target. There are a number of reasons that firms overpay for acquisition targets. First of all, uncertainty about the true underlying value of the target is compounded by information asymmetries between the target and the acquirer. In the extreme, a target may over represent its potential value to suitors. This uncertainty creates a potential "winner's curse" where the party with the most overly optimistic valuation of an uncertain target wins a bidding war. When two firms are bidding on a target, an "escalation of commitment" may occur where firms continue to bid up the price of a target, paying selective attention to supporting information, rationalizing past behavior, and refusing to give up and admit defeat. Finally, some firms have expressed concerns that executives and investment bankers are incentivized to make suspect deals either to reap large fees in the case of bankers or to grow revenues in the case of executives.

How do we use it?

Step 1. Analyze strategic benefits.

The first and most challenging part of an acquisition analysis is assessing the strategic benefit of making an acquisition to the acquiring firm. We define the strategic benefit as the discounted stream of future cash flows generated by acquiring the targeted firm. At the very least, these are the cash flows that would accrue to the acquiring firm if the targeted firm remained an independent operating unit. Hopefully, however, the targeted firm will create value beyond this once it is integrated into the new firm. There are number of potential sources of such added value:

Efficiency gains. By consolidating the operations of the targeted firm and the acquirer, redundant functions may be eliminated and other cost savings may be realized. The acquirer may possess superior capabilities that could be leveraged by the newly acquired firm, or vice versa. For example, the targeted firm could make use of distribution and sales channels present at the acquirer. Alternatively, the targeted firm may have a superior quality program that could be diffused throughout the acquirer. Generally, efficiency gains present themselves in the form of cost savings for the target, the acquirer, or both.

Market consolidation. In the case of horizontal acquisitions (i.e., acquisitions within the same business sector), an acquisition may eliminate a competitor. This, in turn, could reduce downward pricing pressure allowing the new combined entity to increase margins even if combined sales remain unchanged. Note: it is for this very reason that some horizontal acquisitions are disallowed by government regulators who fear the exploitation of market power by firms who gain significant market share. The risk and subsequent cost of prohibited acquisitions should be factored into your analysis.

Complementarity gains. The targeted firm could add value by creating complementarities between the target's product lines and capabilities and the product lines and capabilities of the acquirer. A classic example would be the acquisition of new technologies and intellectual property through an acquisition. Cisco Systems has been particularly successful in acquiring entrepreneurial ventures with novel technology and wrapping them into its existing product lines. Other examples include Disney's acquisition of Pixar in animated pictures and Best Buy's acquisition of the Geek Squad in electronic retail.

Business diversification. Acquisitions are frequently pursued as a way to access new, attractive markets. As with any diversification strategy, one should consider the value or synergy created by occupying multiple business segments. How does the firm's position in this new market add value to existing units? How do the firm's existing businesses add value to this new market position? These benefits may be along the lines outlined above (e.g., efficiency or complementarity gains). Alternatively, it may simply be that possession of a broader portfolio of products and services adds value for customers increasing their willingness to pay for the firm's products and services.

Pulling it all together, we can express the strategic benefits to acquisition as follows:

$$\text{STRATEGIC BENEFIT} = \text{VALUE OF INDEPENDENT TARGET} + \text{VALUE ADDED THROUGH ACQUISITION}$$

Of course, placing solid numbers to these strategic benefits is challenging. A sensitivity analysis is absolutely critical. Consider not only the best-case scenario but also the worst. How difficult will it be to realize various efficiency gains or synergies? What are the chances that the acquisition could destroy value? For example, could the acquisition make the targeted firm worse off than it was prior to acquisition? What is the potential that the talent in the target firm leaves after acquisition? Consider how long integration will take. If we think of strategic benefits in terms of discounted future cash flows, when will positive cash flows from the acquisition be realized? What is your discount rate?

Step 2. Estimate acquisition price.

In this step, you will estimate the acquisition price necessary to secure ownership of the target. As discussed above, this will likely be at a premium over the current valuation of the firm by its owners—otherwise, why would they sell? For publicly traded firms, the valuation is reflected in its stock price and its overall market capitalization. This, in turn, reflects the stock market's current expectation of the stream of future cash flows to be generated by the firm (discounted by the weighted cost of capital). For privately held firms, assessing the owners' valuation of the firm may be more difficult. In venture-capital-backed firms, looking at prior rounds of funding will provide a snapshot of the firm's valuation at the time of investment.

Ultimately, you will need to analyze for yourself the expected future cash flows of the firm given the data available. This is the "value of independent target" discussed above. You may have different expectations than the market or current owners about the future prospects of the firm. If you think the potential to create future value is greater than the current owners do, a firm may be able to acquire a target at less than its assessed value, even ignoring the value added through acquisition.

Another consideration is whether there are other active suitors of a target. This raises the risk of a bidding war and an escalation of commitment as discussed above. Each suitor may have an independent assessment of the target's value if it remained independent and the value added through acquisition. Typically, but not always, the suitor with the highest expected strategic benefit will win a bidding process.

Step 3. Assess opportunity cost.

With estimates of strategic benefits and purchase price in hand, one would be tempted to move forward if the strategic benefits exceed the purchase price. This is a necessary but not sufficient condition. As a final step, you should assess the opportunity cost of investing in the acquisition. Are there other strategic investments that could better achieve the desired objectives of the acquisition? For example, could a diversification play be better achieved through internal development—innovating new products and cultivating new markets in-house? Could complementarity gains be achieved through an alliance rather than an acquisition?

When considering these other opportunities, it is useful to think about transaction costs.[vi] Transaction costs refer to the costs of engaging in exchange beyond the purchase price. For instance, the transaction cost of buying an automobile is the time and effort spent searching, negotiating, and finalizing the purchase. Transaction costs also include the potential costs that arise when a party to an exchange acts opportunistically, taking advantage of a relationship, such as when a potential transaction cost to an R&D alliance is one of the partners stealing intellectual property to use on its own products exclusively. There are a number of potential sources of such opportunistic behavior. First and foremost, when one party to the exchange makes investments in assets specific to that exchange, it opens itself up to a holdup by the other party. This problem can be compounded when it is difficult to separate the effort of multiple parties in an exchange (e.g., in a joint development project). Uncertainty about future contingencies that arise may further compound transaction costs.

In strategy, analyzing potential transaction costs is useful to evaluate the relative costs of producing internally and sourcing externally (e.g., choosing between an acquisition versus an alliance). Many transactions that take place within a firm might instead take place with an external actor. Consider the trend in outsourcing over the past decade. When does it make sense to own a set of activities and when does it make sense to contract with others for those activities? The answer to this question relies partly on the risks inherent in relying on an alliance versus an acquisition. An acquisition implies ownership and imparts "residual rights of control" (i.e., it provides a choice of course of action when unforeseen contingencies arise and creates common incentives and mechanisms for coordination, thus minimizing market transaction costs). On the flip side, ownership through acquisition may increase bureaucratic costs incurred when coordinating layers of management and could lead to slow, inflexible decision making.

To illustrate, consider Disney's purchase of Pixar in 2006 for $7.4 billion. One potential alternative course of action for Disney was to try to develop its in-house computer animation capabilities. How difficult and costly would this have been? Prior to the purchase, Disney had an exclusive marketing and distribution alliance with Pixar. Another opportunity cost of this acquisition was a continuation of the existing alliance. There were a number of strategic benefits to this arrangement: It reduced Disney's costs and its exposure to failed movies, and it allowed Pixar to focus its efforts without the oversight of a large corporate entity. But there were also risks. For one, analysts feared that as a new round of negotiations commenced, Pixar would have a strong bargaining position given its long run of successful children's movies and Disney's increasing reliance on it for new characters and merchandising opportunities. Pixar could potentially charge Disney an exorbitant fee to continue the relationship—an example of the holdup problem. What if Pixar was bought by a competitor of Disney's? What potential costs would Disney incur if it lost the Pixar relationship?

In general, when assessing opportunity costs, consider one or two alternatives and analyze the strategic benefits of those options. Use the most attractive of these alternatives as the opportunity cost. With this estimate in hand, you now have all the pieces to reach a decision and make a recommendation. Simply stated, the strategic benefits minus the purchase price should be positive and should exceed the opportunity cost.

STRATEGIC BENEFIT - PURCHASE PRICE > OPPORTUNITY COST

As mentioned earlier, putting numbers to these constructs can be challenging. You will want to do an extensive sensitivity analysis. It may be useful to identify a break-even point. At what purchase price will strategic benefit minus purchase price equal opportunity cost? Your numerical analysis is useful only to the extent that the underlying assumptions ring true. In general, you want to do your due diligence; evaluate targets inside and out. It is prudent to recognize that there is a high probability of failure with any acquisition. What assumptions about the benefits of integration are you making? How difficult will this integration be to achieve? Successful acquirers work hard at integration. Consider the following rules of thumb: (1) keep debt amount low to moderate—avoid becoming over-leveraged, (2) pursue friendly rather than hostile takeovers—acquisitions where the targeted company welcomes being acquired, (3) consider "dating before you marry"—get to know the acquisition target through an alliance or other business dealings, and (4) focus on how the target enhances the acquirer's core capabilities.

|||||||||||||||||||||||||||||||||||||||||||||||||||||||||||||||||||||||||||||||||||

FOUNDATIONAL READINGS

Foerster, Stephen R., and Dominique Fortier, "Note on Mergers and Acquisitions." Ivey School of Business, 1995.

The Handbook of Mergers and Acquisitions. Edited by David Faulkner, Satu Teerikangas, and Richard J. Joseph. New York: Oxford University Press, 2012.

Hitt, M. A., J. S. Harrison, and D. R. Ireland. *Mergers and Acquisitions: A Guide to Creating Value for Stakeholders.* New York: Oxford University Press, 2001.

Lang, L. H. B., and R. M. Stulz. "Tobin's Q, Corporate Diversification, and Firm Performance." *Journal of Political Economy* 102, no. 6 (1993): 1248–280.

14. Scenario Planning

What is it?

Scenario planning is a process of constructing a range of plausible futures to use as a backdrop for discussing strategies. The most important and most uncertain of the factors are used to generate multiple scenarios of the future. These futures are distinct from one another and are not intended to be treated as specific point forecasts. The core of the process involves illuminating the key predetermined environmental factors or trends and the critical environmental uncertainties. Predetermines are factors such as demographic trends that may be certain within the relevant timeframe, while uncertainties are environmental factors that will have the biggest influence on the success of the decision and whose outcome is uncertain.

When do we use it?

Scenario planning can be helpful at different points in a strategic analysis. It can be used early in the process in a generative way to spur creative strategy identification. Conversely, it can be used after a strategy has been developed to test its robustness against a range of alternative futures.

Why do we use it?

The key benefit of scenario planning is greater sensitivity to the unfolding nature of the future. Most organizations make decisions based on point forecasts, which are single predictions for an element of the future. In fact, many organizations have implicit "official futures" composed of a set of shared point forecasts about the future. Scenario planning is useful because it forces individuals to step outside their assumptions about the future and recognize that many things that they consider to be predetermined are actually uncertain.

Thus, scenario planning prevents groupthink developing around a single possible future.

In a sense, scenario planning facilitates contingency planning for multiple possible futures and heightened recognition of the context of an approaching future. Scenario planning offers a way to have a group conversation about a decision whose success depends upon an uncertain future. It operates on the principle that for some decisions, thinking in terms of multiple possible futures or scenarios is more effective than relying on single-point forecasts of the future. Decisions influenced by multiple sources of uncertainty or where a high-consequence, low-probability event might significantly influence the outcome are well suited for scenario planning. Well-crafted scenarios create a wind tunnel for designing strategies that are robust across the most important and most uncertain environmental variables and are responsive enough to anticipate and adapt to the realization of the future.

How do we do it?

Step 1. Gather information.

Generating effective scenarios is the cornerstone of the entire process. Effective generation requires up-front information gathering and brainstorming, utilizing both the scenario participants and knowledgeable outside parties to develop stories of possible future worlds.

The process begins when an organization has identified a key issue or strategic decision that must be made in a highly uncertain environment. An organization can ask itself, "What specifically are we concerned about with respect to the future?" Examples of questions faced by an organization include: "How will people purchase my company's goods in the future? How will technology affect my manufacturing capabilities? What will changing environmental laws mean to my business?" These are just a sample of the questions an organization might ask before developing scenarios.

An appropriate time horizon must reflect session goals and organizational needs. Time horizons set far enough in the future that uncertainty is important and not so far that hope becomes dominant work well. Organizations may conduct sessions for periods as short as one year or as long as twenty years. Organizations most often use scenario planning for periods beyond five years, although periods less than five years are beneficial for high-uncertainty situations and for organizations considering significant investments or facing paradigmatic change. The best time horizons introduce uncertainty into the conversation without causing participants to disengage from the process because they cannot relate to the scenarios. Time horizons must also reflect economic cycles and industry cycles, such as the approval process in the pharmaceutical industry.

In the second step, the key trends and uncertainties that will determine the way the future evolves are identified and researched. Oftentimes, these things will concern the future behavior of the organization's customers, suppliers, or competitors. Data gathering should focus on unearthing predictable trends, such as population demographics. Observed change, supportable evidence, and expert consensus characterize predictable trends. Scenarios must include the trends in a manner that keeps the focus on the uncertainties. Interviews should focus on unearthing the uncertainties and providing insight; guided brainstorming around the focal issue is the most effective method. The final portion of the data-gathering phase is brainstorming key uncertainties with the participants. One method that allows complete creativity is to have each participant individually write significant environmental factors on post-its and stick them to a wall.

Step 2. Structure scenarios.

Having identified the issue, time horizon, and key trends and uncertainties, the process now moves to prioritization of the latter in a way that will set the stage for the identification of a set of distinct scenarios. At this point in the process, the focus shifts to distilling those crucial elements that will allow the construction of discrete build scenarios. After highlighting the environmental factors, participants must narrow the list to the most critical forces. By identifying the key factors that are most important *and* uncertain, the scenario planner can form the axes around which the differences in the scenarios will pivot. The uncertainties can now be placed upon one, two, or three axes. In this way, the scenario planner can construct a number of different stories (called "logics" or "plots") based on the intersection of the different uncertainties.

The most commonly used approach is the 2 × 2 matrix method, which uses two different outcomes from each of two uncertainties to generate four different scenarios. The uncertainties used in this approach should be as close to mutually exclusive as possible. Each quadrant is a scenario that should be given a memorable name.

Step 3. Write scenarios.

Scenario writing follows the data-gathering and scenario-structuring phases. Scenarios must be vivid descriptions of a plausible future; they are the most effective manner of creating a vision in the participants' minds of the future worlds. Creating stories with vivid descriptions, key headlines, and memorable anecdotes enables participants to envision future worlds in which they may operate while helping them distinguish between the various worlds.

With the uncertainties established and possible futures identified, the next step is generating details of the future worlds. One simple and effective method is generating newsprint headlines as a small group. The group should write headlines they would expect to see 20%, 50%, and 100% of the way into the time horizon in each scenario. The final step of scenario writing is filling in the details; it is the most creative stage—writing the story. The stories should focus on the criteria above and consider the trends consistent with the chosen time horizon. Weaving in the discussion from the brainstorming with the headlines ensures a rich vision.

Step 4. Use scenarios.

After the process of defining an issue, uncovering critical uncertainties, and constructing multiple scenarios, the most critical value-adding step remains of asking: "What are the implications for the strategy of the organization?"

||||||||||||||||||||||||||||||||||||||||||||||||||||||||||||||||||||||||||||||||

FOUNDATIONAL READINGS

Liedtka, Jeanne, Carl Garrett, Vikas Chawla, James Winninger. "Scenario Planning," UVA-BP-0501 (Charlottesville, VA: Darden Business Publishing, 2007).

Schoemaker, Paul J. H. "Scenario Planning: A Tool for Strategic Thinking." *MIT Sloan Management Review* (Winter 1995): 25–40.

PART 4.

Putting It All Together

15. Strategic Analysis in Practice

Recall the strategist's challenge articulated in Chapter 1: to balance the intersection between values, opportunities, and capabilities to create and sustain value for the organization's various stakeholders. Each of the frameworks in this toolkit helps provide insight into some important aspect of these three critical factors. But like the old proverb about the blind men touching various parts of the elephant, each framework provides only a partial picture of the strategic landscape. This means that when an analysis employing only one framework is conducted in isolation, you risk reaching an incomplete analysis of the path forward for the organization.

The key to a successful strategic analysis is to *integrate* across the tools in the toolkit to synthesize findings into a detailed picture of values, opportunities, and capabilities of the firm. Below, we outline a simple four-step process to conduct a robust strategic analysis. Each step is informed by a set of questions to answer that may be supported by one or more tools from the toolkit. These steps address the strategist's challenge: identify the organization's mission and values, analyze the competitive environment, and analyze the competitive position that derives from the organization's capabilities. The final step of analyzing and recommending strategic actions is where all the pieces come together to consider, analyze, and ultimately recommend a course of action for an organization.

Step 1. Identify Mission and Values.

This is a critical and often underappreciated step in a robust strategic analysis. The mission and values provide direction for an organization. They help define an organization's scope and the markets the organization interacts in or may be likely to interact in. Understanding mission, values, and purpose provides direction as to what strategic direction the senior leadership may be willing to pursue.

For many organizations being analyzed by a third party, identifying their mission and values can be slightly trickier. It may be as simple as looking at the company website or annual report; however, be aware that the underlying mission and values of another organization may not be reflected in its official mission statement or in a prominent public listing of a firm's core values. Instead, you may need to probe deeper, looking at the proclamations of the chief executive or examining past behaviors to truly discern mission and intent.

When analyzing your own organization, things should be clearer. Mission and values should be lived at your organization. If the values and purpose of your firm are unclear or difficult to articulate, this represents the most fundamental challenge the organization faces: to achieve clarity regarding values and purpose. And even if your firm's mission is well understood, you may want to engage in a process of devising or revisiting its mission and values statements. This is often the first step in a formal strategic planning process. A stakeholder analysis (Chapter 6) may prove especially valuable when setting or revisiting mission and values. Understanding the myriad of stakeholders who are impacted and impact the organization—what they value and what they expect from the organization—can inform your mission and values.

Step 2. Analyze the Competitive Environment.

Analyzing the competitive environment is critical for identifying strategic opportunities and for beginning to understand the organization's unique value proposition. Using the language of SWOT, analyzing the competitive environment provides clues to the *opportunities* and *threats* facing the organization.

An analysis of the competitive environment should answer some fundamental questions:

- What market or markets does the organization compete?
- Who are the key organizations competing in these markets?
- Is this an attractive market, generally speaking? Why or why not?
- What broad trends are impacting these markets?
- Are there barriers to competition?

- How is the competitive structure of the market likely to evolve?
- What is the nature of the competitive game being played?

Each of these questions can be answered in part by applying the various tools in Part 1 of the toolkit. Competitor analysis (Chapter 1) aids in the specification of the markets an organization competes and in the identification of the various competitors. Environmental analysis (Chapter 2) helps illuminate the larger forces impacting the competitive market of interest, and how such forces will affect how the market is likely to evolve by identifying industry trends that may impact growth and demand. Five forces analysis (Chapter 3) further sheds light on market attractiveness by revealing the underlying competitive structure of the industry and, in particular, whether there are barriers to competition. Competitive life cycle analysis (Chapter 4) provides further insights into how competition is likely to evolve over time and helps reveal the fundamental nature of the larger competitive game being played; for example, whether it is a winner-take-all-market or if there are significant first-mover advantages.

By analyzing these questions using the frameworks outlined in Part 1, the strategist can begin to identify attractive value-creation opportunities. It is important to remember that attractive opportunities are not only driven by demand but by competition. A fast-growing market may seem attractive on the surface but is likely to be a brutal competitive arena if there are low barriers to entry and little opportunity for differentiation. Similarly, a niche position in a staid market could be quite lucrative if there are significant first-mover advantages or entry barriers that keep competitors at bay.

Step 3. Analyze Competitive Position.

Having analyzed the competitive environment of the organization, now we turn our attention inward. It is important to recognize that there are often multiple unique opportunities for competitive success within any given market. The answer to the question of whether an organization should pursue a specific competitive position is driven only in part by the attractiveness of that opportunity. Equally important is whether the firm has the capabilities—or could develop the capabilities—to successfully seize that opportunity to create value. Using the language of SWOT, we need to analyze the *strengths* and *weaknesses* of the organization.

Analyzing an organization's current and future competitive position requires answers to a series of fundamental questions:

- How does the organization deliver value for its various stakeholders?
- What are the unique resources and capabilities that allow it to deliver this value?
- Does the organization have a competitive advantage?
- How sustainable is any advantage the organization may have from these capabilities?
- Can the organization leverage these capabilities across markets to improve its position?

Each of these questions can be answered in part by applying the various tools in Part 2 of the toolkit. Stakeholder analysis (Chapter 6) aids in identifying the organization's value proposition, not only to customers but to *all* the firm's stakeholders. Capabilities analysis (Chapter 7) identifies the organization's unique resources and capabilities that drive its value proposition and helps answer whether a competitive advantage is sustainable. Strategy maps (Chapter 8) can aid an analysis of capabilities by comparing the focal organization to its rivals. Finally, portfolio planning matrices (Chapter 9) can help identify how competitive advantage may be created by leveraging positions across multiple markets.

By analyzing these questions using the frameworks outlined in Part 2, the strategist can identify the current competitive position of the organization and assess whether the organization possesses a competitive advantage in this position. By combing our analysis of the competitive environment (Step 2) with our analysis of competitive position (Step 3), we can begin to assess the overall attractiveness of the organization's position—the intersection where opportunities meet capabilities.

Step 4. Analyze and Recommend Strategic Actions

Our final step is the most critical. This is where we bring together values, opportunities, and capabilities. Given the opportunities in the competitive environment; given the capabilities that may or may not provide competitive advantage to the organization; and given the values and purpose of the organization, the organization is poised to take action. How should the organization position itself in the market? Note this is not simply an assessment of the organization's current competitive position, this is an analysis of where it *should* position itself. Here we are asked not only to understand the current state of the organization but also to be prospective—to look forward and make recommendations for future strategic action.

Answering this question requires a dynamic lens. We need to not only understand what opportunities exist today but ask which opportunities are likely be available in the future. We need to not only understand the organization's current capabilities but ask what capabilities the organization may develop in the future. Ultimately, we must ask how the organization can secure and sustain favorable positions in the future, all the while remaining true to the core values of the organization.

For for-profit firms, this question often manifests itself in the eternal quest to grow earnings. Recognize, however, that many firms have put themselves on the short road to collapse by overstretching in the pursuit of growth. The answer to this question is one of balancing between values, opportunities, and capabilities. Values are paramount here. What is the vision for the organization and how does that inform the opportunities worth pursuing, and at what cost? How will the organization create value for its stakeholders?

Ultimately, the pursuit of favorable strategic positions in the future comes down to specific strategic actions. Should you recommend pursuing an acquisition of another organization in an attempt to gain entry into a new market? Should you recommend investing in R&D to pursue a new market opportunity in your existing market? Should you engage in a price-cutting strategy in an attempt to undercut rivals and gain market share?

The tools in Part 3 of the toolkit provide aid in answering these questions. Consideration of future strategic actions is ultimately a process of hypothesis testing (Chapter 10), where recommendations are advanced, considered, and tested. Payoff matrices (Chapter 11) may help in understanding the competitive interplay that often determines whether a given strategic action will elicit a particular response from a key competitor. Real options analysis (Chapter 12) is a tool for assessing the value of keeping your options open and of having strategic flexibility in the face of uncertainty and actions by your competitors. Acquisition analysis (Chapter 13) provides guidance on one of the most common and challenging strategic actions—mergers and acquisitions. Finally, scenario planning (Chapter 14) is a tool for envisioning multiple hypothetical futures and for assessing the potential outcomes of various strategic actions.

Either individually or together, this set of tools helps in analyzing strategic options to help lead to an action plan for moving the organization forward.

From Analysis to Execution

By following these steps that help you integrate the various tools in the Strategist's Toolkit, one can conduct a robust strategic analysis of an organization. Such an analysis can be invaluable for:

1. A business executive looking to grow a firm's earnings.

2. An entrepreneur exploring market opportunities for a nascent venture.

3. A management consultant providing advice to a client.

4. A financial analyst making investment recommendations.

5. A nonprofit organization looking to differentiate itself in a crowded marketplace.

And for many others. The key is to experiment with the frameworks to see which ones yield important insights and then to consider them together. Pursuing an integrative approach, balancing between the values and capabilities of the organization and the opportunities presented by the competitive environment, the frameworks of the toolkit can help facilitate key strategic insights.

It is important to note that a robust strategic analysis is still only the first step in executing a winning business strategy. While we reserve the term "strategic analysis" to refer to the assessment of strategy, strategic management refers to the process by which strategy is formulated *and then implemented* within an organization. While strategic management is ultimately the responsibility of the top managers of an organization, its execution often involves many levels of the organization and may include internal and external parties such as suppliers, customers, and consultants. Both formulation and implementation are important aspects of strategic management. Strategy can be emergent and is often the realization of both intentional strategy formulation and tactical responses to unexpected stimuli encountered by the organization as it acts on those plans. So while Michael Porter argues that strategy is not merely operational effectiveness,[vii] neither is it solely armchair theorizing and strategic planning.[viii] Strategic management is a dynamic endeavor that involves both content and process, both planning and action.

Common Terminology in Strategy

A

Absorptive Capacity – a firm's ability to assimilate new knowledge based on the firm's prior related knowledge

Acquisitions – an arrangement in which the assets and liabilities of the seller are absorbed into those of the buyer

Adverse Selection – (1) the tendency for those that are most at risk to seek various forms of insurance, or (2) precontractual opportunism that arises when each party cannot freely observe the other's net benefit

Appropriability – the degree to which a firm can extract value from an innovation

Arrow's Information Paradox – in the market for information, to accurately value a piece of information, that information has to be fully revealed to a potential buyer

B

Backward Integration – when input sources are moved into the organization

Barriers to Entry – industry characteristics that reduce the rate of entry below that which would level profits

Barriers to Imitation – characteristics of firm resources and capabilities that make them difficult to duplicate

Barriers to Mobility – factors that prevent the movement of firms across strategic group boundaries in response to profit differences

Bertrand Competition – a model of oligopolistic competition where output is not differentiated and competition is based on price; suggests rents are competed away even with two firms

Boundaries – the scope of firm operations

C

Capabilities – the combination and use of firm resources to produce action

Capabilities Analysis – an assessment of the likelihood that a firm's resources and capabilities will provide a sustained competitive advantage relative to competitors

Cartel – a group of firms that explicitly agree to set prices and/ or to limit output

Causal Ambiguity – situations where competitors are unable to understand clearly the link between resources and capabilities and competitive advantage

Collusion – when firms coordinate actions so as to gain market power over consumers

Common Property Goods – resources to which everyone has free access

Competitive Advantage – characteristics of a firm that allow it to outperform rivals in the same industry

Competitive Dynamics – the series of advantage-seeking competitive actions and responses taken by firms within a particular industry

Competitive Groups – clusters of firms within an industry that share certain critical asset configurations and follow common strategies

Competitive Positioning – the choice of strategies and product segments within an industry

Competitive Rivalry – the intensity with which two or more firms jockey with one another in the pursuit of better market positions

Competitive Scope – the extent to which a firm targets broad product market segments within an industry

Competitor Analysis – an assessment of a firm's competitors' capabilities, performance, and strategies

Complementarities – a group of assets that work together to mutually support a particular strategy

Complementary Assets – those assets necessary to translate an innovation into commercial returns

Concentric Diversification – a move by a firm into related, yet distinct, lines of business

Conglomerate – firms that are in multiple, unrelated lines of business

Core Competencies – the subset of a firm's resources and capabilities that provide competitive advantage across several businesses

Corporate Strategy – strategies by which firms can leverage their position across markets to garner economic rents

Cost Leadership – the ability to produce products at the lowest cost, relative to competitors, with features that are acceptable to customers

Cournot Competition – a model of oligopolistic competition where prices are set by the market and competitors decide output; suggests economic rents greater the fewer firms within the industry

Cross Elasticity of Demand – percentage change in the demand for one good in response to a 1% change in the price of a second good

D

Decision Tree Analysis – a tool for assessing the payoffs to strategic actions under uncertainty and rivalry

Differentiation – the ability to provide value to customers through unique characteristics and attributes of a firm's products

Diversification – the process by which a firm moves into new lines of business

Diversification Matrices – a range of tools for understanding the scale and scope of the firm based on the potential of individual businesses and the ways they influence one another

Divestiture – selling off assets of the firm

E

Economic Rents – returns in excess of what an investor expects to earn from other investments of similar risk (also called above-average returns)

Economies of Scale – unit costs decline as output increases

Economies of Scope – costs of production of two lines of business run together are less than the sum of each run separately

Efficient Market Principle – "when markets are efficient, good situations do not last"

Elasticity of Demand – percentage change in demand in response to a 1% change in the price of that good

Entrepreneurship – the development of new products and processes (i.e., innovation)

Environmental Analysis – an assessment of the elements in broader society that can influence an industry and the firms within it

Escalation of Commitment – sticking to a course of action beyond a level that a rational model would prescribe

Excess Capacity – the capacity to produce additional units without substantial incremental costs or additions to fixed capacity

Exit Costs – costs incurred when a firm exits a business (e.g., early payments of contractual obligations such as salaries or environmental cleanup costs)

F

First-Mover Advantages – advantages held by a firm by virtue of being the first to introduce a product or service

Five Forces Analysis – an assessment of an industry's profitability by analyzing the intensity of rivalry among industry competitors and the threats posed by new entrants, buyers, suppliers, and product substitutes

Forward Integration – when output outlets are moved into the organization

Free Riding – not paying for a nonexclusive good in the expectation that others will

Friendly Takeover – an acquisition where a target firm welcomes offer from acquirer

G

Game Theory – the formal analysis of conflict and cooperation among intelligent and rational decision makers based on the actions available to them and the associated future payoffs

Governance – the structure of inter- and intra-firm relationships

H

Hierarchy – the organization of authority and decision making within a firm

Holdup Problem – when one who makes a relationship-specific investment is vulnerable to a threat by other parties to terminate that relationship so as to obtain better terms than were initially agreed

Hostile Takeover – an acquisition where target firm resists the acquisition

I

Industrial Organization View – perspective that above-average returns derive primarily from industry characteristics that reduce competitive pressures within industries

Industry Life Cycles – the periodic evolution of markets spurred by innovation and technological change

Information Asymmetries – when one party knows more than another

Institutions – various nonmarket stakeholders such as the government, advocacy groups, communities, and unions

International Strategy – the logic behind production or sales of products in markets outside the firm's domestic market

J

Joint Venture – independent firm created by joining the assets from two or more companies

K

Keiretsus – networks of closely linked firms that share equity, common in Japan

L

Learning Curves – reductions in the unit costs associated with cumulative, life-time experience in an activity

Leveraged Buyout – a restructuring action whereby a party buys all the assets of a public firm and takes the firm private

Licensing – when a firm authorizes another firm to manufacture or sell its products (in return for a royalty typically)

Limit Pricing – holding prices lower than what is profit-maximizing in the short term to deter entry

M

Market Leader – a firm with significant market share who may set prices for the rest of an industry

Mergers – an arrangement in which the assets and liabilities of two or more firms are integrated into one firm

Minimum Efficient Scale – the smallest output for which unit costs are minimized

Minority Equity Investment – purchase by one firm of a noncontrolling, minority stake in another firm

Monitoring – an activity whose aim is determining whether contractual obligations of another party have been met

Monopoly – a market with only one seller

Monopsony – a market with only one buyer

Moral Hazard – (1) the tendency for those who obtain some form of insurance to take more risk, or (2) post-contractual opportunism that arises when actions are not freely observable

Multipoint Competition – when firms compete with one another across multiple markets

Mutual Dependence – when two firms have relatively similar amounts to gain from an alliance

N

Negative Externalities – unpriced costs imposed on one agent by the actions of a second

Network Externalities – when the value to a customer of a product increases as the number of compatible users increases

Niche – a specialized part of the market, often small

Nonequity Alliance – contract between two or more firms that does not involve equity sharing

O

Opportunism – when an individual takes advantage of an information advantage so as to pursue his or her own self-interest

Opportunity Cost – the value of the next best opportunity which must be sacrificed in order to engage in a particular activity

P

Payoff Matrix – a tool for assessing the payoffs to individual strategic actions given likely competitor responses

Principal-Agent Problem – the potential for opportunism by an agent when a principal who wants the agent to engage in some behavior has difficulty observing the agent's behavior

Public Goods – resources that are nonrival (marginal cost is zero) and nonexclusive (people cannot be excluded from consuming)

R

Real Options – investments that enable (but do not require) future strategic actions

Rent-Producing Assets – resources and capabilities that confer above-average returns

Reputation Pricing – slashing prices in response to market entry to establish a reputation for being a fierce competitor

Residual Rights Of Control – the right to determine the use of firm assets in the absence of contract specifications

Resource-Based View – perspective that above-average returns derive primarily from within the firm via valuable and rare resources and capabilities that are hard to imitate or substitute for

Resources – inputs into a firm's production process—may be tangible (those that can be seen and quantified) or intangible (e.g., reputation, knowledge)

S

Scenario Analysis – a tool for making strategic decisions in the face of multiple uncertainties by aggregating those uncertainties into a limited set of coherent future outcomes

Schumpeterian Competition – a theory of competition proposed by Joseph Schumpeter in which innovation (not efficiency) is the hallmark of market-based economies

Specific Assets – assets that have value only in a very narrow use

Spillovers – knowledge gained by one agent may be observed by another agent

Stakeholder Analysis – an assessment of the pressures relevant constituencies (stakeholders) bring to bear on a firm

Stakeholders – the individuals and groups who can affect and are affected by the strategic actions of a firm

Strategic Actions – (1) individual actions to meet strategic mission and strategic intent, and (2) actions that require significant resource commitments

Strategic Alliances – partnerships between firms in which their resources or capabilities are combined to pursue mutual interests

Strategic Groups – clusters of firms within an industry that share certain critical asset configurations and follow common strategies

Strategic Intent – a plan to leverage a firm's internal assets to accomplish the firm's goals

Strategic Mission – a statement of a firm's unique purpose and the scope of its operations in product and market terms

Strategic Plan – a synthesis of analyses into a set of future strategic actions for the firm

Strategy Map – a tool for identifying strategic groups and unexploited niches within an industry

Switching Costs – one-time costs customers incur when buying from a different supplier

SWOT Analysis – a general assessment of the strengths and weaknesses of a firm and the opportunities and threats of the firm's industry

Synergy – the excess value created by businesses working together over the value those same units create when working independently

Synergy Trap – overpaying to acquire a firm in the pursuit of synergy

T

Tacit Collusion – when firms take actions so as to gain market power over consumers without explicit agreements

Tactical Action – strategic action that is easy to implement or reverse (e.g., pricing)

Theory of the Firm – an attempt to explain the boundaries of firms by viewing a firm as a nexus of contracts where residual rights of control are maintained

Tightly Held Assets – assets that are both rare (not widely possessed) and are hard to imitate or substitute for

Transaction Costs – cost of carrying out a transaction or the opportunity costs incurred when an efficiency-enhancing transaction is not realized

V

Value Chain Analysis – a tool for identifying a firm's value-adding resources and capabilities

Vertical Foreclosure – vertical integration that cuts off a competitor's access to the supply chain

Vertical Integration – the process in which either one of the input sources or output buyers of the firm are moved inside the firm

W

Winner's Curse – the winner of an auction is the player who has the highest valuation of the asset and thus likely overvalues the asset

Strategy Analytics

MEASURES OF INDUSTRY DEMAND AND STRUCTURE

Item	Equation	Common Uses
Compound Annual Growth Rate (CAGR)	CAGR = (Ending Value Beginning Value) $^{\wedge}$ (1/#years)-1	Useful for summarizing the effect of fluctuating growth rates over several years for items such as revenues
Elasticity of Demand	ED = (% Change in Sales)/(% Change in Price)	Useful for assessing the effect of price changes on demand when setting prices and predicting sales
Cross Price Elasticity	CPE = (% Change in Sales if Good A)/(% Change in Price of Good B)	Useful for assessing the degree to which consumers are willing to substitute one product for another
Concentration Ratio—4 Firm (CR4)	CR4 = Σ Market Share of the four largest firms in an industry	A simple metric to evaluate the extent to which an industry is dominated by a few key firms
Herfindahl-Hirschman Index	HHI = Σ (Market Share) $^{\wedge}2$	The sum of the squared market shares of all firms in an industry. This is a more comprehensive metric to evaluate the extent of concentration in an industry. In a monopoly, the HHI will be 1 (100%)^2 and in a highly fragmented (and presumably highly competitive) industry, the HHI will approach zero.

MEASURES OF FINANCIAL PERFORMANCE		
Item	Equation	Common Uses
Return on Assets (ROA)	ROA = Net Income/Total Firm Assets	A measure of firm performance that makes for clearer comparison of performance among firms that have different amounts of leverage (different ratios of debt to equity)
Return on Equity (ROE)	ROE = Net Income/Shareholder's Equity	A measure of firm performance that looks only at what shareholders are receiving in return for keeping money tied up in the firm
Return on Sales (ROS)	ROS = Net Income/Sales Revenue	A measure of firm performance that makes for clearer comparison of performance among firms that operate in different ways (e.g., among firms where some own the assets they use and others contract for these assets)
Price Earnings Ratio	PE = Price per Share of Stock/ Earnings per Share of Stock	Useful for comparing stock prices among largely similar firms
Free Cash Flow	FCF = net income after taxes less investments in equipment and working capital plus depreciation and any other noncash charges (e.g., amortization of goodwill)	The cash a firm brings in during a year that is not needed to support the firm itself
Discounted Cash Flow (DCF)	$DCF = \Sigma \, (\text{Free Cash Flow})/(1-\delta)^t$	Net present value (NPV) of future net cash flows. Useful for assessing the assumptions required for economic viability of specific strategic actions. (δ is the discount rate to be applied to the project, t is the amount of time until each cash amount is received.)
Market-to-Book Ratio	MB = (Stock Price x Total Shares Outstanding)/Accounting Value of the Firm's Assets Net of Debt	Used as a way to judge if the stock market believes the firm will create more value by operating than it could by selling off its assets
Tobin's Q	Q = (Stock Price x Total Shares Outstanding + Outstanding Debt)/ Replacement Value of Firm's Assets	Used as an alternative way to judge if the stock market believes the firm will create more value by operating than it could by selling off its assets (attempting to correct for accounting)

TOOLS FOR INFERENCE AND DECISION MAKING UNDER UNCERTAINTY

Item	Equation	Common Uses
Break-Even Analysis	B = Fixed Costs/(Price – Variable Costs)	Identify the volume needed to make a project viable at a given price or (less often) the price needed to make a project viable at a given volume.
Decision Trees	See Excel—TreePlan	Identify the best choice today given a sequence of uncertain outcomes and costly or irreversible alternative choices, or identify the value of information that reduces the uncertainty or delays the choices.
Sensitivity Analysis (Tornado Charts and Monte Carlo Analysis)	See Excel—Crystal Ball	Evaluate the range of likely outcomes given that multiple (largely independent) uncertainties can cancel each other out or amplify the effect of one another and identify key uncertainties to be concerned about or areas where changes can have large beneficial effects.
Optimization	See Excel—Solver	Determine how to allocate resources given a varied set of resources and a large number of ways to use those resources.
Regression Analysis	See Excel	Determine how various factors are related from a jumble of historical data. (How great are the scale economies?)

Gathering Strategic Intelligence

Dow Jones Factiva. You can check for articles in major publications such as the Wall Street Journal, BusinessWeek, or even in relevant trade journals using Factiva (http://global.factiva.com/), a database that contains full-text articles for regional newspapers, magazines, press releases, and newswires. The company "Snapshot" under the Companies/Markets tab in Factiva provides Reuters business descriptions and Datamonitor analytics.

Lexis-Nexis Academic Universe. Much like Factiva, Lexis-Nexis (http://web.lexis-nexis.com/universe) can be helpful for identifying news articles from U.S. regional newspapers, magazines, trade publications, news-wire services, and major international newspapers. In addition, Lexis-Nexis provides access to SEC filings, company summaries from Hoover's, and company financial ratios for the past three years. You can also access biographical information, U.S. federal and state court cases, law review articles, U.S. patents, and legal cases from a selection of countries.

Mergent Online. Mergent Online (http://www.mergentonline.com) is a very useful and comprehensive database containing detailed financial information and highlights, company histories, and data on joint ventures and alliances. The database has direct links to EDGAR for public filings. Mergent Online can be a useful if you are interested in information on a firm's board of directors, key personnel, and institutional shareholders. You can also research company earnings estimates and Mergent Online's own equity research reports.

Mergent Horizon. Mergent Horizon (http://www.mergenthorizon.com) can be quite useful in providing stakeholder data, such as financial and other data for a focal firm's suppliers and customers. In addition, the database contains a Merger and Acquisition Scenario Report Builder function, allowing you to see what a hypothetical merger or acquisition between two public firms would look like, with a particular focus on overlapping and complementary product lines and key business relationships.

Research Insight. This database requires special software installed only on select workstations in research libraries. Research Insight gives you access to the Compustat database, the most comprehensive source of financial data available on market-traded firms. It provides annual, quarterly, and monthly financial information, ratios, growth rates, line of business, monthly stock prices, and other market data for over 10,000 active public companies that trade on U.S. exchanges and 7,000 companies that no longer file with the SEC.

SDC Platinum. This database also requires special software installed only on select workstations in research libraries. SDC Platinum focuses on initial public offerings, venture capital, private equity investment, and mergers. For instance, it provides information and data on all types of new security issues, including both equity and debt issuance.

Bloomberg Financial Markets. This database is only available on Bloomberg terminals in research libraries. Bloomberg provides real-time and historical data on a wide range of investment vehicles including stocks, bonds, commodities, currencies, indices, etc. You can access price and other data on international securities, recent newswire articles and press releases, information about corporate executives and directors, and features that allow you to compare securities.

Investex Plus. Thomson Research's Investex Plus (http://research.thomsonib.com/gaportal/ga.asp) gives you access to analyst reports on particular firms by various contributors and analyst information on industries.

CareerSearch. While typically used as a tool for job hunting and career services, CareerSearch (http://www.careersearch.net) can also occasionally help when doing strategy research—especially for smaller firms that are difficult to find in the larger research databases. CareerSearch contains information about companies from a number of company directories and database providers, including CorpTech, Grey House Publishing, Thomson Financial Publishing, and Thomson Nelson.

About the Authors

Jared D. Harris (harrisj@darden.virginia.edu) is on the faculty of the University of Virginia's Darden School of Business and is a Senior Fellow at Darden's Olsson Center for Applied Ethics. He is a celebrated professor who teaches both the required first-year strategy course and the required first-year business ethics course, for which he also serves as course head. He earned his PhD at the University of Minnesota's Carlson School of Management after a distinguished business career, first in consulting at several leading public accounting firms, followed by a stint as a CFO for a small technology start-up based in Washington, DC.

Professor Harris's research centers on the interplay between strategy and ethics, with a particular focus on the topics of corporate governance, managerial decision making, and organizational trust. His work has been published in *Academy of Management Review, Organization Science, Journal of Business Venturing, Business Ethics Quarterly, Strategic Management Journal,* and *Journal of Business Ethics,* and he is the coeditor of *Kantian Business Ethics: Critical Perspectives* (Edward Elgar, 2012) and *Public Trust in Business* (Cambridge University Press, 2013). Harris serves on a number of journal editorial boards, and his work has been highlighted in the *New York Times,* the *Washington Post,* and the *New Yorker,* as well as other media outlets in the United States, Canada, Germany, India, Portugal, and the United Kingdom.

Michael J. Lenox (lenoxm@darden.virginia.edu) is the Samuel L. Slover Professor at the University of Virginia's Darden School of Business. He is an award-winning professor who teaches and serves as the course head for the required first-year strategy course in the MBA program—a course he has taught for over 14 years: first at NYU's Stern School of Business, then Duke's Fuqua School of Business, serving as course coordinator from 2002 to 2008, before joining Darden in 2008. In addition, Professor Lenox has taught over 100,000 students through his massively open online course (MOOC) "Foundations of Business Strategy."

Professor Lenox also serves as Associate Dean and Executive Director of Darden's Batten Institute for Entrepreneurship and Innovation and serves as the faculty director for the multiple-university Alliance for Research on Corporate Sustainability. He received his PhD in technology management and policy from the Massachusetts Institute of Technology and his BS and MS in systems engineering from the University of Virginia. He has served as a visiting professor at Harvard, Stanford, Oxford, and IMD.

Professor Lenox's primary expertise is in the domain of technology strategy and policy. He is broadly interested in the role of innovation and entrepreneurship for economic growth and firm competitive success. He has a long-standing interest in the interface between business strategy and public policy as it relates to the natural environment. His research has appeared in over 25 refereed academic publications and has been cited in a number of media outlets including the *New York Times,* the *Financial Times,* and the *Economist.* In 2009, he was recognized as a Faculty Pioneer by the Aspen Institute and as the top strategy professor under 40 by the Strategic Management Society. In 2011, he was named one of the top 40 business professors under 40 by *Poets & Quants.*

Endnotes

i. This chapter was adapted from Jared D. Harris, Michael J. Lenox, Jeanne Liedtka, and Scott Snell, "Introduction to Strategy," UVA-S-0183 (Charlottesville, VA: Darden Business Publishing, 2010), which was based on an earlier technical note (UVA-S-0166) by Ming-Jer Chen, Gregory B. Fairchild, R. Edward Freeman, Jared D. Harris, and S. Venkataraman.

ii. Kenneth Andrews, *The Concept of Corporate Strategy* (Homewood, IL: Richard D. Irwin, 1971).

iii. Sharon Oster, *Modern Competitive Analysis* (Oxford: Oxford University Press, 1999), 11.

iv. Douglass North, *Institutions, Institutional Change, and Economic Performance* (New York: Cambridge University Press, 1990).

v. Much of this note is adapted from the work of R. Edward Freeman, Jeffrey Harrison, and Andrew Wicks, *Managing for Stakeholders* (New Haven: Yale University Press, 2007).

vi. In 1990, Ronald Coase received a Nobel Prize in Economics "for his discovery and clarification of the significance of transaction costs and property rights for the institutional structure and functioning of the economy." Coase's research and the subsequent work of Oliver Williamson and others form a branch of economic thought referred to as "transaction cost economics."

vii. Michael E. Porter, "What is Strategy?" *Harvard Business Review* 74, no. 6 (November–December 1996), 61–78.

viii. See Gary Hamel and C. K. Prahalad, "Strategic Intent," Harvard Business Review 67, no. 3 (May–June 1989), 63–76; or Henry Mintzberg and Alexandra McHugh, "Strategy Formulation in an Adhocracy," *Administrative Science Quarterly* 30, no. 2 (June 1985), 160–97.